The Library of Pastoral Care

TITLES ALREADY PUBLISHED

IN PREPARATION

Other volumes are planned

Library of Pastoral Care

IN HIS OWN PARISH

IN HIS OWN PARISH

Pastoral Care
through Parochial Visiting

KENNETH CHILD

Hon. Canon of St Edmundsbury and Ipswich
Rector of Thurlow and Rural Dean of Newmarket

LONDON

S · P · C · K

1970

First published in 1970
by SPCK
Holy Trinity Church
Marylebone Road
London NW1

Made and printed in Great Britain by
William Clowes and Sons, Limited
London and Beccles

SBN 281 02345 X

To

Jane

with love

Wherefore consider the end of your ministry towards the children of God . . . in Christ

THE ORDINAL (B.C.P.)

Contents

Acknowledgements

Thanks are due to the following for permission to quote from copyright sources:

Blackfriars Publications: *Revolution in a City Parish*, by G. Michonneau.

Hodder & Stoughton Ltd: *Odd Man Out*, by Eric James.

S.C.M. Press Ltd: *The Church of England 1900–1965*, by Roger Lloyd; *A Ministry Renewed*, by Gordon E. Harris.

Sheed & Ward Ltd: *The People's Priest*, by Cardinal Heenan.

The Editor, *Sunday Times*: Extract from an article on Jimmy Savile, 14 January 1969.

Foreword

There are, I believe, a few clergy who need convincing of the importance of "visiting" as a vital part of the cure of souls in any parish.

I doubt if there are any laity who do. If there are, I have never met them. Indeed I can only record my experience as a bishop that, when discussing with churchwardens or P.C.C. a possible future incumbent, I cannot remember a single case when I do not hear: "he must believe in visiting . . ." or "yes, the last man was a good preacher, bishop, but he didn't visit. . .".

This basic feeling of the need for what some would prefer to call "visiting" rather than the more grandiloquent "personal encounter" springs from an innately right conception of the role of the parish priest. It is truly biblical.

The author is fully aware of the developments in pastoral psychology and the new horizons opened up by clinical psychology, but he is endorsing the claim of Roger Lloyd that we should not forget "that distinctively Anglican characteristic, the emphasis on the office of a pastor, and the primacy of this office over that of the prophet, the scholar, or the administrator".

As with his previous book, *Sick Call*—about the Pastoral Care of the Physically Ill—Kenneth Child does not write as one who "knows the answers". But the reader, whether experienced priest or newly ordained deacon, will immediately recognize that the conversations recorded and the people described are real, to be met in parishes all over the country.

All through the book the author shows his complete awareness of modern conditions, whether dealing with the telly, the shifting population, the overlarge and understaffed parish, or the present climate of theological opinion. And I was encouraged by his chapters entitled "We visit as specialists—as prophets—as servants—as listeners".

Perhaps the most attractive characteristic of the whole book is the feeling inevitably conveyed to the reader that the priest who comes out of the pages is doing this part of his divine commission, however dreary or difficult it may seem at times, with real love and a devotion to people, caring for them, wanting to know them, for God's sake.

How often as ordinands or young priests we were told to do something but given too little instruction about how to do it. This book provides just that about "visiting"—pastoral care; and it does so at a time when the parish priest and his job are under fire from many quarters. Many, old and young, will be encouraged by it.

✠ GEORGE GUILDFORD

Preface

I was honoured by being asked to write the first volume in the Library of Pastoral Care. That was a little book about the care of the sick and some people have been good enough to say kind things about it. Now I have been asked to write about pastoral care in the parish in its most basic form, that of parish visiting.

I have written these pages with the greatest diffidence because I am only too conscious of my own failures and inadequacies in respect of pastoral care in the parish. So many times, too, have I said in criticism of a brother priest who was engaged in diocesan or central church activity that "he ought to spend more time in his own parish". Now, alas, one finds oneself making up one's diary with (not unwelcome, one must admit) commitments which will excuse one from "routine visiting".

Moreover, perhaps we have all acquiesced of late in the devaluation of parochial visiting which manifold changes in the structure of church life have forced upon us. At the same time I have a suspicion that it may be that we have not always seen "visiting" in the context of the whole life and mission of the parish priest. It is certainly true that the newly ordained deacon or priest in his first assistant curacy will never see his daily visiting in true perspective unless he sees it against the background of his priesthood as pastor, prophet, and servant.

The pastoral side of our task as clergy is fairly obvious; we have hesitated about our "prophetic" ministry; we are only just coming to terms with the truth about the "servant concept" in regard to our ministry. I shall attempt to suggest ways in which all these three aspects can be seen to combine in the day-to-day visitation of his own parish by the faithful parish priest.

The older and more experienced clergy will find some parts of this book naive—let them remember that it is not really written for them. Rather have I put myself in the position of a young deacon or priest who is tackling for the first time the problem of caring for the hundreds or thousands of people "in his own parish".

I should like to express my gratitude to all my friends in Lancashire, London, and Suffolk who have provided me with much of the material in this book. More especially do I crave the forgiveness of my parishioners in Newmarket who were neglected during the writing of it.

Great Thurlow   KENNETH CHILD
Suffolk

1

Parish Visiting

"Of course, parsons don't visit nowadays...
I remember the old Vicar, he was always
around...came to tea almost every Thursday...
I think he liked my scones."

The situation is a familiar one to the parish priest who has
spent many years coming to grips with the problems of
parish visiting. The new curate has knocked on the door of
42 Winchester Way, in the hope of getting to know the
family of a confirmation candidate. It is about 2.15 p.m.,
and the father of the family, who is on the early shift at the
local mill, is in his slippers and shirt sleeves, watching television. He answers the door and the first thing he notices is
a clerical collar; he plots an escape route very rapidly and
unloads the problem of a slightly unwelcome visitor (he is
waiting anxiously for the starting prices for the two o'clock
race) on to the shoulders of "mother" who, he feels,
normally looks after the spiritual interests of the family.

"Ah, yes, I'll call the wife", and he quickly shows the
clergyman into the front room. "She won't be a minute—
she's upstairs with the baby." He then goes to the bottom of
the stairs and shouts with a voice unnecessarily loud,
"Mother! The curate's come to see you about Christine."

Father returns to the other room and his television, and
the young pastor is left to study the photographs and
presents from the sea-side on the mantelpiece as he waits
for Mother, who had overheard the husband's greeting and
immediately dashed upstairs to straighten her hair.

Many young priests are filled with dismay after a few
visits such as this. They feel that they would be more
profitably employed in some other way, although they may
be at a loss to explain what "some other way" might be;
and they find themselves listening gladly to older priests
who will maintain that the apparent lack of "results" from
parish visiting hardly justifies the expenditure of time and
energy involved.

When Mother does finally come downstairs she has
obviously "put her face on" in haste and is a bit flustered.
It is at that moment, probably unthinkingly, that she utters
the remark about "parsons not visiting nowadays" and
in her embarrassment exaggerates the previous vicar's
addiction to scones.

The young pastor, a little incensed at the remark and not
a little impatient with the attitude of the household, may
be tempted to write the visit off as a waste of his time. Let
him be more patient and after a few more visits, if he has
a modicum of common sense, he will be able to walk into
the house, sit in the back room and watch the television
with Father, and talk about the latest bit of news or something a Bishop has said, while Mother does the washing-up
with her hair in a state of glorious disarray.

This little book has been written in the firm belief that
pastoral care in the parish must involve in great measure
the visiting of people in their homes. We believe that the
priest, if he is to fulfil his ministry as pastor, prophet, and
servant must be as much at ease in the homes of his
parishioners as he is in his own study or his own pulpit.

The impatient curate, inwardly fuming in the front room
of 42 Winchester Way, would do well to meditate upon the
words of Roger Lloyd:

In the Anglican way of life what really counts is the
cumulative pressure upon society of the anonymous host
of the average; and certainly the Anglican Communion

believes that its own particular part of the Kingdom of
God will best be occupied and won for Christ by the
rank and file membership of the Church. Our real heroes
are those whose names can never be known, the ordinary
parish priest, the Sunday School teacher, the member of
the Mothers' Union, the sidesman, and most of all the
small band of the faithful who make the congregation at
the Eucharist on weekdays.[1]

We plead for dynamic leadership, we hanker after new
theologies, we long for a re-structuring of the machinery of
church government, we strive for liturgical up-to-dateness:
but we should not forget

that distinctively Anglican characteristic, the emphasis
on the office of a pastor, and the primacy of this office
over that of the prophet, the scholar, or the administrator.
One could argue for ever whether this scale of compara-
tive values is just or unjust. The point is that this is how
Anglicans instinctively think or feel—how they *must*
think or feel if they are to lay all the responsibilities of
heroism upon the anonymous and obscure average of
churchpeople of all races and languages.[2]

[1] Roger Lloyd, *The Church of England, 1900–1965* (S.C.M.), p. 20.
[2] *Ibid.*, p. 20.

2
What do we mean by Pastoral Care?

"The use of the term 'pastoral' may seem to need some
explanation, if not justification, in view of the pejorative
associations ... so often attached to it in these days."[1]

THE PASTORAL MEASURE

In June 1967 the National Assembly of the Church of
England completed its consideration of "The Pastoral
Measure", a piece of legislation which amended or annulled
countless other Measures and Acts of Parliament. It was
primarily the work of a Commission which had been working for many years on the codification and revision of legislation relating to "pastoral reorganization". It is a weighty
document, full of legal language and technicalities about
such things as the union of benefices and pastoral "schemes".
The whole matter was debated for hours and hours in the
Church Assembly and members of both Commission and
Assembly breathed a great sigh of relief when, having been
passed to the Ecclesiastical Committee of Parliament, it
received the Royal Assent in May 1968.

Within its many pages one looks in vain for any clear
definition of "pastoral care"—rather does it deal with the
machinery for making more flexible and effective the framework in which pastoral care is to be exercised in the Church.
The cynic may speculate as to what effect on the life of the
Church there might have been if all the man-hours spent on
the production of this measure had been devoted to active

[1] *Partners in Ministry* (C.I.O. 1967), Section 4, p. 18.

pastoral care in the parishes. Such speculation would be meaningless (and we should be the first to admit that the Pastoral Measure *was* necessary), but the fact that such speculation does take place ought to remind us that the very word "pastoral" is in danger of being devalued and misunderstood. For example, it was something of an absurdity that a Diocesan Pastoral Committee was recently informed that the actual pastoral visiting in a certain parish was not the concern of the Committee.

It is true that the parish priest should welcome the developments in pastoral psychology and clinical pastoral theology which have widened the horizons immeasurably for priests who are trying to help their people in situations which may have been unknown or, more probably, unrecognized, a generation ago. But there is a danger that these fields of pastoral care may be elevated into such exciting subjects for discussion and experimentation that the ordinary day-to-day "shepherding" work of a priest is forgotten or disregarded as being pedestrian and "unprofessional".

Again, while it is true that pastoral care in its widest sense is also the concern of the psychiatric social worker or the official at the Ministry of Social Security, the parish priest still retains his responsibility for the "cure of souls" in his parish—he is still the "shepherd of the parish", he is still responsible for the pastoral care of God's children in Christ and is responsible *to* the Great Pastor, the Good Shepherd himself. We are only pastors because we are servants of the *Pastor Pastorum*.

PATERNALISM

As we drew towards the end of the 1960s we were able to look back on a decade when the clergy found themselves being satirized, analysed, and organized as never before except during a full-scale persecution of the Church. It all started with that marvellous sermon of Alan Bennett's in

"Beyond the Fringe". After the initial shock we found our-selves playing a tape recording of it at the beginning of training courses for would-be "television parsons".

Then came the uncomfortable diagnosis of Leslie Paul when we were even more shocked at the impropriety of having a lay sociologist to pinpoint our shortcomings. We began to be very sensitive about what we came to think of as the "image" of the clergy.

We survived all this and are no doubt all the better for it. But we have become all too self-conscious about the pastoral office. Perhaps we may quote from Section 4 of *Partners in Ministry*, the report of the Fenton Morley Commission, which was appointed as a result of the Paul Report (C.I.O., 1967):

> The use of the term "pastoral" may seem to need some explanation, if not justification, in view of the pejorative associations ("a shoulder to weep on") so often attached to it these days. The Commission does not mean by "pastoral" the kind of paternalism which modern man, "come of age", understandably resents: nor does it, in the non-pejorative sense, regard the exercise of such over-sight as the prerogative of the clergy. The Commission has in mind getting to know a man as a person, putting oneself alongside him, becoming sensitive to his unique situation. . . .

It is difficult to see the real point of such language. Modern man, whether he is "come of age" or not, who is to be found in the streets and flats and pubs of our land in 1970 will certainly reject the "paternalism" of the parson who self-consciously and deliberately forces himself "along-side", but he will certainly not reject—and indeed will respond to—the pastoral care which is the reflection of the paternalism of the God and Father of us all. But let it be a paternalism which cares and does not patronize; which cares, not from the "big house" but from the chair by his fireside . . . not from the Town Hall but at the same bar in the "local" ... if we *must* get alongside him, let it be in the queue at the fish and chip shop.

"Hello, John. How are you getting on? Wife all right?"

"Fine, Rector. You've never been to see us. We're all fixed up in the new flat now."

"Well, can I come up now? Better late than never."

"Sure, come up. I've just been to the post. Margaret's not in—she's gone round to her mother's with something."

"These lifts all right? They have a reputation for breaking down."

"They'd be all right if people used them properly ... here we are—this is us. Let me put the light on."

"But you've got it nice and comfortable. I'll sit here ...

No, don't switch the television off ... oh! it's that programme there's all the talk about."

"I thought you might be a bit shocked at some of it."

"No, I'm not really. I know it shocks some good people a lot, but I think there's a lot of truth in it. Old so-and-so's ideas are very common, you know."

"Margaret and I enjoy it very much, but she thinks it goes too far about the Queen and the Government, and it makes cracks about religion, too. I didn't think you'd like that."

"It does take my breath away sometimes, I must admit. But so does the New Testament when you really get down to it!"

"Well, you know more about that sort of thing than we do, really. ... Would you like to hear the tape recording of our wedding? We often play it ... do you remember, you let us plug Margaret's brother's tape recorder into that socket by the organ?"

The visiting priest endures the embarrassment of hearing his own voice expounding "the causes for which matrimony was ordained" and the nervous repetition by the bride and bridegroom of the tongue-twisting words "till death us do part".

> "Must say, I was blooming nervous—although I was in the choir at school and I used to sit in those choir stalls at the Carol Service. . . . We were wondering the other night whether you expected us to come to church."

> "Well, I don't think I could say that I was *expecting* you to come . . . but I should be very thrilled if you both *did* come."

> "Mary's been confirmed, I think, but I never got round to it. I don't really understand it. And you hear so much on the telly these days about religion that you don't know what to think."

How well the experienced pastor knows the opportunities —and the pitfalls—of that kind of visit! But one could hardly describe this kind of "reasoning together" as paternalistic. It is probable that at the beginning of our ministry a generation or so ago we had as our heroes the giants of the past who stumped round their parishes, whose word was law, and who by their very frown brought recalcitrant members of their flocks to the altar on the following Sunday morning. It might even be that some of us still try to behave towards our people as if we were still in league with the squire or mill-owner, but we know deep in our hearts that if we would be true pastors, we must, with Pope John XXIII, "persuade ourselves that our fellows are always superior to us, and that they are therefore worthy of the greatest respect".[1]

John and Margaret came to confirmation classes together. John was confirmed. God alone will judge whether it was

[1] *Journal of a Soul*, paperback edition, page 178; Geoffrey Chapman.

"paternalism" or "getting alongside" which brought them into the worshipping fellowship of the Church.

PASTORAL REORIENTATION

In a stimulating essay on "Faith, Works, and Value" in his *Essays in Pastoral Reconstruction*,[1] Martin Thornton asks the question, "Whatever the motive behind it, what is 'making the Church attractive' but a clever display in a shop-window, what is most 'visiting' but a party canvass?"

Father Thornton takes no pains to disguise his own dislike of parochial visiting but goes on, in a later essay—"1984"—to overplay his hand with some rather wild arithmetic which could inject sheer defeatism into the minds of young priests with a real, pastoral sense.

> Whatever the principle and motive behind total systematic visitation, whether it is or is not a worthy pastoral plan—all that is beside the point, for it just cannot be done. We have already reached the stage when single-handed priests are responsible for 25,000 souls; some are loyal to the visiting tradition and "do their best", which means that by heroic labour they seriously visit 20 people a week, or 1,000 a year. Together with all the modern administration, organization, committees, and so forth, that is a remarkable achievement; but it would take 25 years to visit the parish, and this on the false assumption that everyone remains in the same place. Apart from more serious factors, modern instability is itself enough to undermine the visiting method, and in any case I fail to see what a visit every 25 years is supposed to achieve. On an annual basis this arduous and heroic labour has achieved 4 per cent of the planned system, but 4 per cent of a system means that the system has broken down.[2]

This analysis sounds quite devastating, but, if one is realistic in one's thinking, probably half of the 25,000 will

[1] S.P.C.K., p. 83.   [2] Ibid., p. 88.

not be Anglicans; moreover, the number of *people* is not half so important as the number of houses or flats. One can reckon that three or four people on average are in one dwelling, and not *many* parishes have that population any-way. The problem, when cut down to size, is not quite so fantastic.

We recognize only too well the wry smile which is appear-ing on the face of many a harassed parish priest, who is single-handed in a parish of 20,000 people or more. The con-stant duties at the cemetery or crematorium, the task of pre-paring people for, and solemnizing, the marriages of up to a hundred couples a year; the eternal war with boilers and church roofs, the fact that in some of our town parishes traditional forms of pastoral care are made impracticable because of the large Jewish or immigrant populations; all these factors cause him to look unbelievingly at what appear to him to be trite statements that we have a distinct pastoral tradition in the Anglican Church and that we are different from other churches in that we have pastoral responsibility for every soul within the borders of our parishes, whether they be Anglican or not.

The reader must believe us when we say that we are not unacquainted with the difficulties. But if "politics is the art of the possible" so perhaps is pastoral work the art of the possible in the situation which the twentieth century forces upon us. What we shall suggest in later pages is, we believe, both possible and practicable.

But it is only practicable if we hold unswervingly to the conviction that pastoral care must involve the knowing of our sheep by their shepherd and the shepherd's being known of them. The great pastors of the past are still remembered in their parishes not so much as paternalistic father-figures but as friends. They did not look for "results" such as crowded churches or successful Stewardship campaigns: they were men of prayer who were known of their people and who understood the folk in their parishes without the bene-fit of consumer research and sociological surveys.

3

First Visits

"Remember, my son, that no human contact is to
be despised. Your first job is to get to know the
family, introduce yourself, and make friends."

We remember very vividly the Monday afternoon a quarter
of a century ago when that piece of valedictory advice was
given to a young deacon who was being launched on his
first voyage in the seas of parish visiting. His clerical collar
still felt rather awkward around his neck after only two
days' wear. The district for visiting which had been allotted
to him had about 1,500 houses in it: he had looked at a
plan of the streets and had a vague idea of which road led
where. He had inserted into the back of his visiting book a
rough sketch plan which would, he thought, help him in his
perambulations. His vicar had supplied him with a list of
people to visit during his first week. The deacon realized
months later that this list had been cunningly compiled—it
was a skilful essay in "sampling"—and many years later he
now recalls with gratitude the details of that launching.

Three hours later he returned to the clergy house for a
quick cup of tea before Evensong, feeling strangely elated
but at the same time saddened by the ordinariness and
tedium of it all. At some houses he had been received with
open arms and made a great fuss of; at others he had
listened patiently to nothing but criticism of the church and
the Vicar; in another house he had been regaled with
eloquent accounts of how much the vicar relied on that
particular household for anything of worth that happened

at the church; in only one house had he tried to deal with what he felt was a "spiritual" problem—the sorrow of a mother whose son was missing off Singapore. And he didn't feel that he had dealt with that situation very expertly.

At the end of three weeks he was welcoming gladly a ruridecanal chapter meeting which would excuse him from the daily round of visiting. And when the verger was taken ill and the vicar asked the deacon to take on the job of stoking the church boilers and supervising the lettings of the parish hall he was overjoyed. Here was something he would *enjoy* doing because he would be able to see results—and, after all, he told himself, it *was* necessary to have a clean warm building for the worship of Almighty God, and one could do church accounts to the glory of God just as much as going to see that feckless mother of one of the choirboys, who never seemed to have changed the baby's nappy when he called.

It needed some stern words from the Vicar to remind him of his prior duty—to get to know and to get known by the people in his "cure".

INTRODUCING OURSELVES

On our first visit we should go to the "front" door, if it is possible. Of course, with flats there is usually only one door possible. If we go round to the back of the house and find a family in the middle of a meal or an altercation with the neighbours over the back wall, there is always the danger of causing needless embarrassment. Later on, when we know the family well and the idea of the parson coming to the back door and being shown through the kitchen with washing hanging around and a table strewn with crockery and milk bottles has become familiar it may be possible for us to become "back door callers".

So we knock on the door or ring the bell. We must be prepared for some wary looks from whoever it is that opens the door. Remember it may be a harassed mother who has to deal with bolts and locks and chains on the front door. Her fingers may be wet from the washing up; her hands may be black from the cooking-stove. Who *are* we, anyway? Even if we think that everybody will know who we are (and, after all, our photograph *did* appear in the local paper when we were appointed to the parish) we should remind ourselves that the sight of a clerical collar on the doorstep is calculated to rouse divers fears and suspicions in the minds of those who open their doors to us.

There are so many people that it could have been! A thief posing as a clergyman, someone trying to sell encyclopedias, a man from a debt-collecting agency. . . . We must put ourselves in the position of the people in the house.

We should introduce ourselves courteously and say "Good afternoon" or whatever it might be. "I'm the Vicar [curate, assistant priest, Rector, parish priest] from St Agatha's. I'm trying to get to know people in the parish. I wonder if I might come in?"

It may not be convenient for us to be invited into the house. After all, they may be dressing to go out; they may have the insurance man in the front room, discussing a new life policy. Or they may say quickly, "Oh well, we always go to St Maxentius'—the Vicar there comes to see us".

We must be polite and say, "Well, it's nice to have met you, Mr (or Mrs) Brown—it *is* Mr Brown, isn't it?" (We shall have elicited this bit of information from the civil register of electors which can be brought from the local council offices). If the Browns have left, this will be an opportunity for us to correct the mistake in our parish lists.

Sometimes, of course, we meet the householder who is incensed by the whole idea of a clergyman appearing at his front door. He may be in his carpet slippers; he looks us up and down and a scornful smile appears on his face.

"You won't get much joy here. We're all atheists."

"I like atheists."

"Aha! A bit of your sales talk, eh?"

"Well, now. What did you *want* me to say?"

It is difficult to remain good-humoured in a situation such as this, when someone is determined to start an argument and is resolved on taking a rise out of the clerical visitor. The good-natured way in which we should take his gibes and parry his shafts will do more for the Kingdom of God than a peevish shaking off the dust of his garden path from our retreating feet.

MAKING FRIENDS

At another house the visit may go like this. After introducing ourselves, we are invited into the house. We sit down. We observe the television set, the wall-to-wall carpeting (synthetic), the sideboard probably handed down from mother, the flying birds on the wall above the tiled fireplace.

"My husband won't be a minute. He's only just got in from the office and he's just finishing his meal."

"Where does he work?"

"In the Accounts Department up at the factory."

"Oh, yes. A lot of people seem to work there. Most of the people I've been to see so far, anyway."

"Do you think you'll like it here? The last curate was very happy here, but I don't think he got on with the Vicar."

"Oh, I think that was just a rumour—we all have to move on sometime."

"We come to Evensong on most Sundays—we like your choir. We haven't been to hear *you* yet."

As the conversation develops and Mrs B prattles on, we begin to feel unutterably depressed inside ourselves and we make savage resolutions to preach a powerful sermon, the next time it is our turn to preach, on the evils of sermon-tasting, the immaturity shown by the choice of a church for the sake of its music, and the sin of gossip.

It is in these moments that we should remind ourselves that it is our duty as Christian pastors not to quench the smoking flax; we should remind ourselves, too, that Mr and Mrs Brown have *not* just finished a course in theology nor have they had all the opportunities we have had of reading all the latest books about Christian discrimination and "taste".

Later, when we are offering Mr and Mrs Brown in intercession at the daily offices we shall perhaps offer our penitence too. We shall perhaps renew our vision of the vocation of the pastor to love the unlovable and admit to ourselves that the unattractiveness of some people and their domestic surroundings is only matched by our own arrogance and intellectual snobbishness.

We shall be humbled, maybe, some months later when Mrs Brown asks us to call and "because there is nobody else I can talk to" tells us that the specialist at the hospital has just told her that her husband has cancer of the liver and has only a few months to live. And we shall marvel at her courage—and faith. It may even appear to us that we ourselves stand in greater need of spiritual direction than she does. And we shall think in shame of that day we were tempted not to bother to call.

"YE ARE MY FRIENDS"

Some of us are better at making friends than others. In a sense, the more shy and retiring we are the better. Nothing is more tiresome than the gregarious young priest who overwhelms his parishioners with "friendship", slaps people on the back and asks them to call him "Tom" on his first visit.

How can we make conversation? Cardinal Heenan has some wise words in his book, *The People's Priest*. It is advice for priests of his communion, but it is no less valid for Anglican clergy.[1]

[1] Sheed and Ward, p. 78.

How can we make conversation? The advice of the Gospel is: Let your speech be: Yea, Yea: No, No. And that which is over and above these is evil." (Matthew 5.37) But the context explains the lesson. Our speech should not be used to curse or revile. On our visits we have to say more than "Yes" and "No". But quite often we can allow the people to do most of the talking. The less we talk the more intelligent we are likely to appear. We shall sometimes find a man alone in his house. A word about what interests him most—it may be his work or sport or politics—and he will deliver himself at great length of his views on the subject. After his ten minutes' monologue the wife may return. He will tell her: "Father and I have had a very interesting conversation". So we need not worry unduly if we are slow of speech and find it easier to listen than to talk. In choosing the right topic before coming to the main business of our call—the spiritual good of the household—a general rule is that men prefer to talk about themselves and women about their family.

Some parishioners will be very inquisitive and will long to know about our social background, where we come from, what college we were at and so on. We should be factual but prudent. It is good if we can point out that we have had a perfectly normal upbringing like anybody else—the superstition still exists that priests are a special breed of human being and have somehow been exempt from the trials and temptations of the adolescent world.

One of the questions we shall invariably be asked is, "Do you think you will like it here? We're a funny lot, you know." In some parts of the country there is to be found a tremendous loyalty to the county or district—or parish ("they are a funny lot over the road")—and we shall remember not to take it too seriously, but always to take it into account.

If there is to be real friendship, there must be trust. Therefore, if we say at the end of a visit "I'll come and see you again" we must see that we do carry out our promise. If we say, "I'll bring you a book about that point we were discussing", let us not forget to take it or send it. If someone tells us something about the noisy habits of their next-door neighbour and the number of empty gin bottles in their dustbin, we must keep that gobbet of information to ourselves and not become known as purveyors of gossip. It may be that we shall put a cryptic remark "Gin?" in our visiting book against the number of the house; when we visit the house a couple of weeks later, it is possible that we shall discover by chance conversation that the bottles had been used for storing distilled water!

Friendship need not involve that kind of "familiarity" which many of the older clergy fear. When people come to know us well they are less likely to be reticent in their conversation—and the same applies to the pastor. But there *is* a danger: as we are treated more and more as "one of the family" we are flattered and we are tempted to let our hair down and behave and talk as if we were back in the common room of the theological college. Familiarity need not breed contempt; it must involve restraint.

During the Second World War a newly ordained curate went to a parish in the north of England where there was a "great tradition"—a great priest had ruled over it for over a quarter of a century in patriarchal manner. The parish had known and flourished under a pastoral care which had been exercised intensively from a parsonage which had been converted into a club for men and boys. The revered Rector was known by everyone for the fact that he never "visited" except in cases of serious sickness or bereavement: but many men and boys owed their conversion to the Christian religion to this singleminded pastor.

When the curate arrived in the parish, economic conditions and social changes had dictated the closing of this club and a new kind of pastoral care—through intensive visiting of the homes of the parish—had taken its place. Complaints were loud, some families withdrew their support

of the church, great bitterness was to be found amongst
many of the men. As the young curate tried to persevere
with his district, constantly he came up against the accusation that "they had closed the Church House and were turn-
ing people away from the Church".

One of the most vociferous opponents of the new régime
was a man of great influence in the parish: his house was
also in the "district" of the new curate, who forced himself
to call regularly even though he knew he would have to
listen to the same old arguments and accusations about
"the new lot ruining the old man's work".

Somehow a friendship was forged and now twenty-five
years later one of the first Christmas cards to drop through
a parsonage house's letter box in the south of England is
from "Frank and Mabel" with a note such as "Thought of
you at the 8 o'clock last Sunday."

"If we have faith in the power of God's grace it is impossible to describe even the most abandoned (or stubborn)
of our flock as hopeless."

4

We must have a System

"You clergy are always talking about
wanting to cooperate with the doctors...
But where are your clinical notes?
You never seem to keep any."[1]

Pastoral care in the parish can never be defined by means
of neat formulae or orderly labelling, but as a doctor must
accept the discipline of detail in regard to the keeping of
records about his patients, so ought we, as pastors, to be
systematic and businesslike about our visiting.

We are only too conscious of the fact that whatever
system we adopt, or suggest should be adopted, some reader
will say, "It wouldn't work in *my* parish". Others may say
that what we are going to suggest belongs to another age
and that new methods are needed. It may be that it is not
as easy to "visit" in the 1970s as it was a generation ago,
but we have a suspicion that priests are so uncertain of their
"role" today that many of them have not even attempted the
old and well-tried methods.

Let us suppose that there are 800 houses in our parish
or "district". Three hundred of those will (on average) be
non-Anglican; that leaves 500 nominally C of E. If we make
twelve new visits a week, we shall have covered our Anglicans in a year. The other three hundred we shall spread
in more leisurely fashion over two years. At the end of our
diaconate we should know the names of everyone in the

[1] *Consultant Physician.*

parish; at the end of our curacy (if it's for three years) we should have been into every house. This sounds slick and rather too easy: for many people this leisurely tackling of the pastoral needs of a parish would seem to lack urgency. But if we would be honest we shall have to admit that rarely in the Church of England is even this kind of modest programme attempted. The enormity of the pastoral demand befuddles us and we take refuge in schemes, campaigns, and movements.

THE VISITING BOOK

Some very proficient parish priests will tell you about efficient card-indexing systems and in cases where there is a parish secretary or the incumbent has that luxury, a secretary, to type his letters and keep his filing system up to date, it is surely the right thing. But for a normal curate or incumbent with a medium-sized parish, the best thing to have is a strongly bound note book about 6 in. by $3\frac{1}{2}$ in. in size. With the aid of a parish map and what parochial records there are, together with a copy of the civil electoral roll, we can compile our visiting book with names and addresses, arranged with the streets or roads in alphabetical order, in the matter of a few hours at the beginning of our first year as a deacon.

It is a good plan to have a system of asterisks and other symbols (or coloured inks, if you want to be so elaborate) to denote whether the folk at No. 9 Windsor Place are C/E, Meth, RC, Agnostic, Moslem, and so on. We might have other symbols to show whether any of the family is a communicant, whether they have the parish magazine, come to Sunday School, Mothers' Union, the Young Wives, etc. It is a help in later years if we leave enough room under each entry for the names of the children of the house as we get to know them. Some priests will find that one word like "Geordie" or "Monty" or "Wm." will be enough to remind us on our next visit that Mr A used to live in Newcastle and we talked about dog-racing at Brough Park, Mrs B had a son who was on Field-Marshal Montgomery's staff in the desert, and that Mrs C had been confirmed late in life by the Bishop of Manchester. It is a feather in our cap if we can recall these things on our next visit. "Fancy you remembering that, Reverend!"

We have known cases where irreverent remarks about one's parishioners were unthinkingly inserted in a visiting book. "This woman is an old bag" was probably not far from the truth in regard to one old gossip, but it would have been a little wiser to have constructed some system of symbols or used Russian for the entry in the book! One embarrassed pastor happened to leave his visiting book in somebody's house one day. No doubt the family in question had some hilarious reading.

On the whole, it is best not to take one's visiting book—certainly not to produce it and write in it—on one's visits. A rough notebook should be used for jotting down information which can then be transferred to the visiting book at the end of a day's foray. This is very important: we should be as scrupulous about this as, no doubt, we are about filling in credit slips at our Bank.

If all the information is carefully and economically entered on the left hand pages of the book, the right hand page can be used for entering the dates of our visits, so that we can check on the regularity of our visits to, say, an invalid or chronically sick person.

After three or four months of careful compilation our visiting book will be in the process of becoming a walking library of information and our natural curiosity, even if we could not claim it was our pastoral zeal, will make us spare no pains to find out some details for the blank space in our book which stands for that curious house with the peeling paint where there is always a light on the top floor and a notice on the front door which says "All big parcels to the back door, please."

There is a familiar dictum of a certain famous parish

priest that the place for the visiting book is not so much on the study desk or in the priest's pocket as on the prayer desk or wherever the zealous priest makes his intercessions. It is certainly true in the writer's experience that many visits have been prompted by the reminder caused by the morning intercession for people in such and such a street of the parish. And what pastor has not been stirred by the account of the parish priest on his death-bed, audibly reciting in his prayers the names and streets from his visiting book?

PRIORITIES

This kind of systematic compilation of one's visiting book must not be an end in itself but ought to be the background of the more intensive "visiting with a purpose" which is or should be going on all the time. Sick calls, visits to homes of confirmation candidates, visits to make arrangements about funerals, parish activities of various kinds are all opportunities of getting to know, and getting to be known by, the parishioners.

Bewildered clergy often ask, "But what do you think are the priorities?" and we are often told by those who write in some periodicals that what the clergy ought to be doing is to leave the ninety-and-nine and go after the "unchurched" or the "unclubbable" or the outcast. "Ought I to bash round my parish seeing Mrs Bloggs who's fallen out with the Enrolling Member of the Mothers' Union or ought I to be doing something about the meths drinkers under the railway arches?"

The writer is as bewildered as anybody about such questions, but we would suggest that the priorities in pastoral care in a parish should be:

1. The dying
2. The sick
3. The bereaved, the depressed, and the anxious

4. The people with whom we have contact through the occasional offices—those who have babies to be baptized, those who come for "churching", those to be married

5. Confirmation candidates and their families

6. "Normal" church members and the "lapsed"

7. Those with no church connections.

Some priests may feel that No. 7 ought to be much further up the list and it may be that with some kinds of "specialized" parochial ministries this kind of categorization is quite irrelevant and unrealistic. All we are suggesting is that for the deacon or new incumbent of a fairly normal sort of parish this *might* be the order of priority.

What is fairly certain is that if we do not have a scale of priorities established in our strategy our visiting will become purposeless and haphazard. We shall lose heart, become frightened by the size of the problem and find ourselves telling our colleagues that "it's a waste of time".

"NO HUMAN CONTACT
IS TO BE DESPISED"

During our first months in a parish we must be prepared to *learn*. We may feel that we have got a lot to give and that our task is to *teach*; we have had an expensive and lengthy education, we are professionally trained and people need *our* help. It is more true to say that we need *their* help in the business of learning to love human beings. The phrase "love of souls" is often used very lightly and we often pride ourselves that we have become possessed of it when we have merely learnt how to get on with people, but loving people as people, and not as potential pew-occupiers, is an art or technique hammered out in the discipline of learning about one's parish or district and learning about people.

The door was open at No. 47 and the priest looked

straight into the living room. A crackly transistor radio was blaring out "Housewife's Choice" and a small, grubby child was crawling on the bare linoleum which was covered with every kind of plastic toy, bits of newspaper, and scraps of food. There was a stench of urine and in the middle of it all, as if presiding, sat an old man in an upright chair.

"Come in, I don't know who you are. Can't move very easily ... I've got rheumatism in both feet now. ... Oh, I see—you're a parson. What do you want?"

"Good morning, sir. I'm from St A's. I was just calling round getting to know people. What are you doing? Baby-sitting?"

"What the so-and-so do you think I'm doing? Suppose you think that's clever. ... Well, if you'd had to put up with the things I've suffered you wouldn't think of standing there all smarmy-like. And what's the bloody church done for me? All you do is draw rents from flaming brothels in London...".

"I'm sorry if I said the wrong thing."

"Wrong thing! You'll never say a right thing as far as I'm concerned. Look what's happened here. My daughter-in-law (she used to be one of your flaming Rose Queens) went off with an American two days ago without a word ... my son's gone off to work and left me with the baby ... her mother won't do anything, the old cow, and...".

Somehow the priest won the old man's trust. There had to be many visits to that house, many telephone calls to welfare officers and children's officers and so on, before the situation was tidied up. The old man retained his dislike for parsons and his prejudices about "the church" until his death, but a few days before his passing, he did say to his daughter, "When anything happens to me, I'd like that young chap from St A's to do the put-away".

THE VANITY OF VISITING

"He used to come here like coming home." It would be foolish to ignore the dangers of over-emphasizing the "visiting" side of pastoral care. The kind of parochial tycoonery which leads a man to rush round and visit "all the houses in my new parish in the first three months" and to have a breakdown if he does not succeed is probably just as self-centred as the attitude of the artistically minded priest who wants to get the décor and the ceremonial right "before I do any work in the vineyard".

If we spend all our time in the houses of our people and ignore the duty of reading, sermon preparation, and service preparation . . . if our church is untidy and draughty on Sundays or if we don't take pains about our "desk work" . . . then is our visiting in vain. And if there is to be purpose about our visiting, there must be system and strategy.

5

Different Kinds of Visits

As often as I have been amongst men
I have returned less a man[1]

Those who spend a great deal of time in doctors' surgeries, psychiatrists' consulting rooms, personnel officers' departments, or the studies and confessionals of clergymen know the intensity of the feeling of being "drained out" at the end of a period of counselling or diagnosing or prescribing. There is also the feeling that perhaps the wrong advice has been given, the sense of having failed to get to the root of a problem, the knowledge that one has overreached one's capabilities in regard to a particular case. Ought one to have had a second opinion?

In a deacon's first year as a pastor there will be many occasions when he returns to the clergy house or the curate's house after a three or four hours' "stint" on the pastoral beat with his mind full of this kind of feeling of inadequacy. Let him take heart! We have all felt it. Wearily, perhaps, he pens the hieroglyphics in his visiting book which describe his afternoon's or evening's labours. Not always is he able to cross-check his findings with an experienced pastor; not always is he able to confide in an understanding churchwarden or trusted layman. He can only commit his day's pastoral stumblings to God.

How different it all seems from the neat, categorized definitions of people which he has in his notes of the pasto-

---

[1] Seneca (4 B.C.–A.D. 65).

ralia lectures at his theological college! How stupid some people are and how unresponsive to the claims of the Gospel! But it may be that it is his own ineffectiveness which has caused him to fail to persuade a single person to be prepared for confirmation? There must be something wrong with his approach ... he had always been given to understand that if you visited madly your church would be full to overflowing on the following Sunday.

It is only after many bouts of introspection such as this that we come to realize that pastoral care is not like a sales campaign producing results which can be illustrated on graphs, but a long and laborious process which has its roots in the heart of God and its fruit in the invisible economy of God's purpose.

What we now propose to describe in terms of conversation are some visits which might be made in four different kinds of parish. The reader may feel that we are falling into the trap of "typing" the human race; the older priest, if he has been patient enough to read as far as this, may feel that we are over-simplifying parochial situations; we are conscious of the dangers—and plead for the reader's patience.

Example 1

House: No. 55

In a terrace next to a fish and chip shop. In fact, the people who keep the shop live here and let out rooms above the shop. Visit in afternoon of Monday when shop's closed. Man and wife just had nap; TV is on.

"Good afternoon, I'm the curate from St A's. I've come to see you."

"Come in, brother. The Vicar said you'd be coming sometime. Glad to meet you. The wife said she'd been introduced to you at church. She goes on a Sunday morning: I like to lie in ... when you've been busy on a Saturday night with this business ... I come at Christmas and

Easter, of course . . . and we do our bit when the little envelopes come round, you know."

"Yes, it came with the magazine this time. I see you've got yours."

"Yes, we advertise in it you know. It helps you—and it comes off my income tax!"

"Yes."

At this stage, the pastor is wondering what his approach should be. The man seems so sure of himself. Why shouldn't he be? Ought the pastor to slip in a cautionary word about "worldliness"? The wife enters and the pastor has to switch his thinking.

"Hello, brother. Sorry I wasn't down here to welcome you, but I've just been upstairs changing. When you're in a business like this you've got to change everything, you know. Otherwise you carry the smell everywhere you go. Switch that telly off, Albert. You can't hear yourself speak!"

"I've been chatting to your husband."

"I expect he's been telling you a load of cod's wallop. You want to get on to him, brother. He won't come to church —says he must have his lie-in, the lazy old basket."

At this point, the pastor is a little disconcerted. If he joins the wife's side, he will probably sacrifice the husband's good will for ever. If he tells the wife not to nag, it might look as if he were not applauding the wife's regularity at church each Sunday. The pastor has to say something. . . .

"Well, you know. I never 'get on' to people. Not yet anyway. I haven't been in this job long enough".

"That's right, brother. Now look—I reckon I'm just as good as all these people who are never away from the church. Gossiping lot, some of them, too. . . ."

The wife is embarrassed by her husband's outburst ... the visiting pastor wonders what the lecturer in pastoralia at his theological college would have done.

> "I don't think this discussion will get us anywhere. Surely what we've all got to do is to follow our consciences. Now you were going to show me your new potato peeler...."

There were many visits after that. There were illnesses, bereavements, financial crises. The priest became the recipient of many confidences about the husband's *affaires* with a girl assistant: he was called in as a witness in a court case when the wife was accused of stealing a packet of frozen peas from a supermarket. He was the celebrant when husband and wife came to the altar together on their golden wedding anniversary.

Example 2

A new Rector was appointed to a country parish with a population of about 250 people. The living had been united with two other small benefices. There had been no resident priest for about two years and services had been taken by a faithful reader and a retired clergyman. The rectory was modernized and redecorated, central heating was installed, the squire sent two of his gardeners down to tidy up the enormous garden, the bishop and the archdeacon descended on the village for the induction and institution, the little church was packed for the service and a crowded village hall was the setting for the "cup of tea afterwards" and the customary speeches of welcome and the usual tearful good-byes by the new Rector's ex-parishioners who had arrived in coaches from the town parish where he had ministered "before his breakdown". After the first Sunday, he began to see the bareness of the land. Congregations were even tinier than he had been led to expect after an inspection of the registers ... there was no choir ... the Rector was expected

to light the coke stoves in church on Fridays so that the
church would have a temperature of 45° on the Sunday. . . .
The new Rector embarked on the visitation of the fifty or so
houses in the village.

"Good evening, Mr . . . er . . . Smith, isn't it? I'm the new
Rector. I thought I would drop in to see you. I hope I
haven't caught you in the middle of your tea."

"No . . . good evening, sir. I'm afraid we don't belong to
your church. We came here from Newtown about six
years ago. The children were christened there and we've
never really changed. The wife's not in—she goes helping at the pub in the evenings . . . I'm sorry she's not in."

"Well, do you think I could come in for a few minutes?
You know, I've only just arrived and I'd like to get to
know people."

"Yes, come in. The place is in a bit of a mess and we
haven't cleared the tea things away yet. The girl's been
watching the television and John's in the front room
doing his homework."

"Oh, don't bother about that. I've got children myself.
Gosh, it's warm in here . . . my glasses always get steamed
up."

"This is Sandra . . . and this is Hilary . . . I suppose you
think they ought to be coming to Sunday School. I've
been on to them about it, but you know what kids are
nowadays. We had to go three times on a Sunday when
we were children."

"Well, Sandra and Hilary, you'll be very glad to know we
haven't got a Sunday School . . . and I haven't really
come round about that. But you'd be very welcome at
church, you know—all of you. There's a lot to do for us
all in this village."

"Mind you, this is the first time we've ever had anyone
from the church to see us."

The wife told all the customers at the pub that the new Rector was going round visiting . . . Sandra and Hilary were confirmed . . . father came along to church for the first time on Remembrance Sunday . . . John (in the front room) always remained rather distant until he went to a university and grew a beard.

Example 3

It's a large, detached house in the "stockbroker" belt of a northern town. There's a swimming pool, a tennis court, and a three-car garage. The well-tended lawn and garden witness to the fact that there is a full-time gardener and that the lady of the house has green fingers. It's lunchtime on a Saturday. The priest drives his 1100 gingerly up the drive and parks it alongside the Alvis.

"Hello, padre. Nice to see you. . . . Come in."

"I'm sorry if this an awkward time."

"No, we're just going to have a snifter. Will you have one, or have I said the wrong thing. Don't know whether you're a member of the Band of Hope or something."

"I'll have a Scotch, please. Nice place you've got here. I haven't been here long . . . oh, water, please."

"Moved here about seven years ago. Television chap had it before me . . . looks a bit Hollywood but it's very pleasant here. When you're in the city all day making your pennies it's nice to come home to a bit of quiet."

"What do you do?"

"I'm in textiles. We're going through a thin time at the moment with all this economic business, but it gives us a living, you know."

"It's one great big mystery to me, I'm afraid. I've seen your wife, I think, at the W.I. Do you have much to do with the village?"

"Oh, yes, we muck in with things. Of course, I'm away a lot, and they're always on to you for a subscription for this or that...".

"Do you ever go to church?"

"Well, frankly, no. I've been at Christmas and Easter and Harvest Festival, but I'm not one of your keen ones. Quite honestly, I'm a bit puzzled about the whole thing. I don't really know what I believe."

"I don't think you're much different from any of us in that respect. I know I've had to hang on by the eyelashes sometimes to the Christian Faith."

"It's good to know that you chaps have doubts sometimes. Some of you always seem so cocksure."

"I wouldn't say cocksure, myself, but I know what you mean."

"I was reading something the other day...".

That man never found a really strong faith, but when he gave a cocktail party at Christmas he invited the priest and his wife. One of his guests, after five champagne cocktails, attacked the young pastor with a long tirade against the church. They became firm friends and now the man organizes discussion groups in various houses in the parish. The priest is coming to the conclusion that these are most fruitful when he is not there.

Example 4

The scene is one of those enormous blocks of flats—"a street on end"—in South East London. The priest is walking along a balcony nine floors up. Children are playing, washing is hanging out to dry... he steps carefully over go-karts and tricycles and goes to the door of No. 145 and rattles the broken letterbox-cum-knocker. He hears the agitated voice of the person he presumes to be the mother saying "Quiet, Angela. There's a man at the door. Go and see who it is. If it's the man about the telly, tell him I'll pay him next week". The door is opened cautiously and a little girl's face peeps out; she sees the priest:

"Mam, it's the Church man."

"Oh! Ask him in."

"Good morning. Is this where Michael Jones lives? Can I come in?"

"Yes, Father. I'm sorry to be like this, Father. Switch that thing off, Angela. She's off school with sickness and diarrhoea, Father."

The large television set which had been exhibiting Test Card C and emitting Latin American music blinks into silence.

"I'll tell you what it is. There's nothing to worry about. But the Chaplain at St X's Hospital gave me a ring this morning. He tells me that Michael's had his operation and is going on fine. We usually keep in touch about anyone from my parish."

"Oh thank you, Father. Thank God it's all over, bless him. I'm going up there this afternoon. It's very kind of you, Father. I don't come to church as I ought to, but with five children and a husband who's only home every few nights. . . ."

"What does your husband do?"

"He's a long-distance lorry driver. It's good money but the children don't see much of him and children need a father, don't you think, at their age, especially Michael— although he's a good boy, but I wish he'd come to Scouts or be in the choir or something. . . ."

There will be many heartbreaks over families like this. Friendly, feckless, their lives conditioned by the advertisements on the television, the pressures of the compressed society in which they live, the longings to move into surroundings where petrol fumes and the sound of electric trains will not provide the background of their lives. But let the priest become their friend as well as their pastor-father.

OUR ATTITUDE

Seneca was no doubt alluding to the danger of losing one's integrity or poise or detachment when he said that he returned less of a man when he had been *amongst* men. The dangers for a Christian pastor lie perhaps in another direction. It is so easy for us to become impatient about what we think are people's stupidities and incompetences; it is easy for us to become "little popes" who bully people; it is easy for us to become the sort of schoolmaster who is more interested in the register of attendances than in the happiness and welfare of his pupils.

Yet we are not welfare workers. We have not the qualifications to be such professionally trained experts, but we shall be no less interested in the material welfare of our parishioners and not be slow to put them in touch with the welfare officers which local authorities appoint. We are not policemen, although at first the children may not be able to distinguish our role from that of Dixon of Dock Green or the school attendance officer. We ought to visit as priests, as pastors trying to extend the friendship of Christ to our people, offering gentleness rather than harshness and believing that sympathy and encouragement will be much more powerful in the end than rebukes and recrimination. And the more we meet people and try to share their lives, the more humble we ought to become. Seneca did not know the *whole* of the story.

Time and time again we must go back to the picture of the Good Shepherd in Chapter 10 of St John's Gospel: "I know my sheep and am known of mine".

6
When to Visit

"Of course you're not like ordinary people,
Vicar, with fixed hours.... I suppose you
could say that you're on duty all the time."

One of the nicest stories about a great Lancashire priest of
the past concerns his unannounced arrival at the house of
one of his flock who had been lax in his attendance at
church. The father of the house was in the middle of his
Saturday midday meal which he was washing down with a
pint tankard of beer. When the voice of the priest was heard
at the door, the man rapidly transferred the beer under the
table where it was hidden by the tablecloth. Besides being a
man of decided ecclesiastical views the Vicar was also not-
able for his teetotal outlook. During the exchange of sharp
words about attendance at the altar, the Vicar's large dog,
which always accompanied him on his pastoral journeys in
the parish, sniffed its way under the table and began to lap
very loudly the glass of beer. The Vicar looked down in-
quiringly, lifted the table cloth and then thundered at the
man, "And so you are revealed ... adding deceit to your
intemperance!"

The writer remembers another great Lancashire parish
priest, Canon Peter Green, laying down rigid rules to the
newly ordained about the way in which their time should
be rationed. The mornings should be reserved for reading
and sermon preparation, the afternoons should be spent
visiting, and the evenings devoted to clubs and organizations. That may have been possible and profitable thirty or

forty years ago, but that kind of rigid demarcation is well-nigh impossible today. In some parishes, where the majority of the women go out to work and the children have their midday meal at school, the only possible time is in the evening. Then, of course, everybody is watching television, and the priest is said not to be welcome because Grandma wants to watch such and such a programme and Julie is piqued if she can't watch *her* favourite. It is possible, of course, for the priest to make an effective pastoral visit without the television set being switched off, although if he is well known and respected the set will be switched off anyway. What we do consider is a discourtesy and a piece of pastoral imprudence is for the pastor to march into a living room and switch off the set himself. We have known certain children to be made lifelong enemies of the church through such thoughtless action!

Somehow we have to thread our way through these difficulties. And there are occasions when it may be profitable to sit through an important news bulletin or programme with a family so that we may discuss its implications in a homely way.

In this, as in regard to all pastoral visitation, we have to be wise as serpents and gentle as doves, and we have to spend a little time at the beginning of the day planning our evening visiting. In one house we know we ought to go *after* 6.30 p.m. to give the man of the house time to finish his tea but *before* 8.30 p.m. because we happen to know that on Tuesdays he always goes for a game of snooker with his son. We shall know, after a quick glance at the TV programmes, that practically everybody in the parish will be watching a beauty competition, say, at 9.5 p.m. on a particular evening and so we shall not visit any house where there is a real, sticky domestic problem that we have been asked about. For good or for ill, we have to learn to live with the "goggle-box".

On some days, it may be that we shall reserve the afternoons for our reading and sermon preparation and spend our morning in parish visiting. A surprising number of older people are at home in the early part of the day. It is in the afternoon that they venture out to visit their friends or go shopping or go to their "Over 60" Clubs.

In regard to the whole of our visiting we must learn to be flexible—and always we shall be courteous. Even in the shabbiest of homes we shall be meticulous about observing the rules of good manners. It may seem unnecessary to say this, but in a day when we seem to be over-concerned with what is called the "image" of the clergy and the Church we are apt to forget that the description "he's a gentleman" may come nearer to the nature of the Good Shepherd than "he's just like one of us, doesn't give a damn for anybody".

"OCCASIONS" OF A VISIT

"No, don't come to the vicarage, I'll bring a form round to your house." This is not said to keep the vicarage door bell quiet or to avoid waking the vicarage baby, but in order that the observant pastor may be able to break new ground. The young mother who wants to have her baby baptized has not been in the parish very long. It took quite a lot of courage for her to approach the Vicar in the street and ask him about Baptism: she had heard that there were some-times difficulties about having children baptized and one neighbour had told her of three cases she knew of where the Vicar had actually *refused* to christen their babies and that they had gone off to another church to have their babies "done".

The Vicar jots down the name and address and in a few days calls in the evening with a Notice of Baptism form and is able to talk quite naturally about the sacrament and the details which the form requires.

"Well, neither of us has been confirmed, actually."

"Yes, well—the opportunity doesn't always come our way in lots of cases . . . but what we always like to point out about the service is that Baptism looks forward to Confirmation. We are always ready to prepare anybody for Confirmation—at any age. I presented a man of over 80 the other day, for instance."

That kind of conversation would not have been possible if the priest had not made capital out of the opportunity presented to him by a chance meeting in the street.

BEREAVEMENTS

The telephone rings. "Is the Rector in?" It is the Co-operative Society's Funeral Department. Mrs X of 17 Lobelia Avenue has just died. They would like to have the funeral at St Ignatius' on Friday—at 2.30 if possible. They would like a hymn and Psalm 23. This sort of telephone call is received in countless parsonages every day. We wonder if the pastoral opportunity is always "bought up" as zealously as it might be.

Let us assume that Mrs X has had no contact with the pastor in her earthly life. The Rector had always understood that she was a Methodist and had not met her (he's only been in the parish for six months.) Before the undertaker rings off the Rector has made a note of Mrs X's age, nearest relatives, where the body has been taken, and when the people are likely to be in. He goes to the house and finds, say, the husband or perhaps the daughter and the son-in-law. He expresses his sympathy and gently and carefully inquires about the circumstances of Mrs X's death. Within the space of half an hour he is acquainted with a good deal of knowledge about the deceased lady, her family, her good points, and sometimes her inadequacies.

In cases of tragedy or sudden bereavement there is often uncontrollable grief and there is need for few words. On other occasions it may seem right to spend quite a long time just listening.

"And now could I just talk over the service?"

"Well, she always said she didn't want any fuss—just a simple service."

"Yes, and you'd like Psalm 23."

"Well, is that the same as something called Crimond?"

The arrangements are completed and the Rector plans his withdrawal.

"Would you like to see her? She looks very peaceful."

"Yes. I should. Perhaps you'd like me to say a prayer."

"Oh, please."

The priest is taken into the front room. The sheet is drawn back and the priest looks at death. There is no room to kneel and so he stands as he says a short commendatory prayer and then, with the rest of the family, if they have come in, the Lord's Prayer.

At the funeral it will be possible to give a short address which "personalizes" the ceremony. It would be grossly hypocritical to say anything which might give the impression that the priest had known Mrs X intimately; it would be equally wrong to preach a panegyric in the style of an eighteenth-century tombstone inscription, but it is perfectly possible to make reference to Mrs X as a mother or a sister or wife in a perfectly natural way, which would be quite impossible if the officiating minister had never been to the house and merely asked the undertaker at the church door (or even during the first hymn) "Is it a man or a woman?"

IT IS NEVER "INFRA DIG" TO VISIT

A quick look at the "Births, Marriages, and Deaths" column in the local paper is never a waste of time. This is the regular chronicle of pivotal happenings in the life of one's parish and the wise pastor will not neglect the information which he may glean from his reading even if it includes some unfortunate doggerel to commemorate Grandfather's third anniversary of death. It can never be amiss for the priest to call to express his sympathy or congratulations. If he goes to call on someone who has just heard that he has been awarded the K.C.V.O., it must be just as important that he calls on someone who is celebrating his 96th birthday or has won a football pool.

The shepherd rejoices with them that do rejoice and weeps with them that weep. It may sound rather trite to talk about "our joys and sorrows" in one's parish magazine, but one is often humbled by the way that people in a closely knit parish do share one another's burdens and one another's triumphs. It is not all backbiting and jealousy.

7

We visit as "Specialists"

> Is it not wisdom to consult Men in their respective Professions as occasion requires and not to go to a Carpenter to fit us with clothes, or to a Taylor to build a house? We ought to have proper remedies ready for every moment of our lives. . . . The remedy is the whole mind of Christ.[1]

On his day off a young priest once doffed his cassock and clerical collar and started to shovel five tons of coke into the cellar of the church boiler house. There were two reasons for this: first, he needed some exercise and his cassock belt was getting rather tight because the clergy-house housekeeper's penchant for the frying pan, and secondly, the verger-stoker had flu. He had no conscious desire to let people see how strong he was or how very "human" he was, but an old man leaned over the church fence for some minutes watching the display of manly brawn and finally was heard to say, "You know, those hands of yours were made for a shovel, not a prayer book".

To this day the priest does not know whether that remark was a compliment or not. Nor does it really matter. We are called, so we believe, and ordained to be ministers of God and we ought to be trained to be pastors and experts in our particular calling or profession. Too often, it would seem, we are prone to excuse ourselves from our primary task and to try to justify our existence by an over-anxious attempt to dabble in every kind of technique which does not belong to

[1] Henry Compton, Bishop of London, 1675-1713.

our office. The deacon is often a little piqued by the gibes of his friends in other professions about "tea-drinking curates" and reacts by diving into every kind of activity which he bravely thinks would make the Church seem more relevant to modern life. The sight of the queue outside the welfare officer's department in the new Town Centre causes the new priest, already disheartened by the apathy and unresponsiveness of his flock, to think ruefully, "If only they would come to ask *my* help". He imagines that a knowledge of social psychiatry would help him, he becomes absorbed in local politics or industrial relations—and the parish suffers.

It would be stupid and unrealistic of us not to admit that some priests have a vocation to work in non-parochial ministries, to do a priestly work in contexts unfamiliar to, and unrecognized by, the "establishment" of the Church until recent years; but there must always be the norm of the parish pastor, not a jack-of-all-trades but a simple, human priest trying to apply the "whole mind of Christ" both to himself and the people amongst whom he has been sent to minister. And there is no one else to do it.

An ex-Army chaplain was helping in a parish for a short time until he was appointed to a living. He took some of the Sunday services; his sermons were short and breezy; he had a good voice and sang well; the choirmaster got on very well with him and some of the older people were even heard to say to him, "We wish you could come here; the Vicar's a bit of a stick-in-the-mud and we don't see much of him".

The Vicar asked him one day to do some visiting in a block of new flats. In particular, there was one young married woman about whom the vicar was a bit worried—her husband had left her, with four children under six.

He went along and found the girl surrounded by four children, a broken-down washing machine, noise and chaos. The young mother looked distraught as the baby of four months had a raging temperature and the doctor had not been for two days although she had rung the surgery three times.

The priest used all his charm and sympathy, mended the fuse of the washing machine, played with the older children, and rang the surgery himself and talked to the doctor, whom he had met golfing the day before. He was feeling genuinely pleased with himself at the change he had wrought in the general atmosphere of the household by the end of the afternoon. The doctor came, put the mother's fears at rest, prescribed penicillin ("with a nice raspberry flavour—she'll love it") and said he would call the next day.

It was over a cup of tea, produced miraculously from a muddle of a kitchen, that the girl said shyly, "How on earth does a person like me say any prayers in the middle of all this?"

Almost blushingly, the priest found himself giving real "spiritual direction" to the girl. This was the hardest part of the visit, putting himself into her position, busy as she was from the moment she got up until the last weary moment of the day. Perhaps the mnemonic A-C-T-S would help her late at night when all the children were asleep and she had done the nappies and the children's clothes. "Adoration— well, just tell God you love him . . . C for confession . . . look back over the day and say you're sorry for anything . . . ("But I feel so bitter about that woman he's gone off with . . .") Let God take your bitterness, he knows all about it—he was let down himself when he was crucified . . . T for thanksgiving . . . there's still a lot to thank God for . . . four lovely children, although they are a noisy lot ("David, stop hitting Jennifer") . . . S for Supplication . . . long word: means asking for things . . . "Or you can pray on your fingers . . . like this. . .".

The priest would still say, years later, that he felt humbled as he left the flat, almost as if he had been to confession himself.

He may discuss the writings of the mystics at his Clerical Society meetings and use highly technical language about ascetical theology and the purgative way, but his mind must often go back to that afternoon of spiritual direction in the most unlikely surroundings of a noisy flat with steamed-up windows.

But why unlikely? Perhaps we may quote Martin Thornton again:

"... to the surprise of many people, it must be pointed out that, by the unanimous consent of all reputable scholars, ascetics is that branch of spiritual theology which deals with the first elementary stages of the Christian life; it aims to serve the needs, not of the gifted zealot but of the weaker brother, not of the mystic in the cloister but of the man in the street. It is not so much concerned with the maximum austerity which the mystics can stand, but with the minimum discipline under which babes in Christ can grow at all...".[1]

Man in the street ... woman in the flat ... babes in Christ ... Henry Compton's words are still relevant: "The remedy of the whole mind of Christ".

[1] *Essays in Pastoral Reconstruction*, S.P.C.K., p. 22.

8

...But also as Members of a Team

"Why are you not saying what you ought to say and saying it with power and eloquence? Why don't you force us to pay attention to you and listen to you? We should like to see you less timid, more consistent, bolder. We often have the impression you are afraid—of what, really? And you spread so little light and joy around you. When you make yourselves heard it is usually with cares, complaints, lamentations, and accusations...."[1]

TEAM VISITING

It is said sometimes that by concentrating on the *pastoral* side of our ministry we avoid the duty of *evangelism*. Rather is it the case that true pastoral care *is* evangelistic in that the gospel is preached through the extending of the Good Shepherd's love and compassion through the mediation of human hearts and hands to individuals. And the more he understands and cares for people the more the priest will long to sound the trumpet for God and the message of salvation in the parochial surroundings in which he finds himself. His mind will turn to projects such as "Missions" or "Conventions" or courses of stirring sermons with provocative titles: he will listen to more experienced priests who will tell him many stories of superhuman efforts made in a particular parish to rouse the people by a mission. "It was all right

[1] Karl Barth in a B.B.C. address.

while it lasted, but after six months we were back where we started."

Others will tell him that the idea of the "old-fashioned Mission" is now out of date and that you can no longer appeal to the residuum of Christian faith that there was in hearts and minds of the masses a generation ago—which is what the famous mission preachers used to count on, or so we are told.

This chapter is not the place to argue the pros and cons of this perennial problem. What we are going to suggest is that it is within the bounds of possibility to make use of many of the techniques of the experts in formalized evangelism inside the limited scope of a medium-sized parish where there is only one priest.

REMOTE PREPARATION

The vicar has been in the parish for eighteen months and has visited diligently the homes of the congregation and other parishioners. He decides that in another year or so the parish would be ready for a "teaching week", or a "children's mission" with sessions for parents. He talks it over with his Parochial Church Council, explaining that he really is unable to tackle anything along these lines on his own. Perhaps he has a week-end retreat with his keener folk: in any case, he will have to have teams of visitors. At this point he would be well advised to have appointed a •Society meetings and use highly technical language about the visitors; if he tries to do it himself he will become a prisoner at his desk. He must be prepared to delegate a lot of the work, and it is quite surprising how the most unlikely people love playing about with lists. Witness the flurry of endeavour in any political party's committee rooms during a General or Local Election.

The week has been fixed, the missioner invited, preliminary announcements made. Groups of people such as religious communities have been asked to pray for God's blessing on this *corporate* effort by the parish. Six or seven months before the date arranged, visiting by teams of two people begins. They will have, say, twenty houses to visit. They are told:

1. You have been selected as a visitor to blaze the trail for the Parish Mission (Convention, Effort, "Get-together Week". . .) next Lent (Holy Week, October . . .) Enclosed with this you will find a small notebook which contains twenty addresses. These houses are your "parish" for the next few months. The success of this campaign or effort will depend largely on *your* care of your parish in preparation for our week (fortnight etc. . .).

2. Visit each house during the next month and take one of the enclosed letters. [These take the form of a simple invitation to come to church with a few details of what is going on.] It is no use dropping it through the letter-box. If there is nobody in, go another day. Say some prayers about it before you go.

3. Be as friendly and courteous as possible with people. Don't argue or lose your temper, but be prepared to answer questions about the church. If people say "Someone has been very ill and nobody's ever been from the church", make a note of it and express your good wishes.

4. A person's manner goes a long way towards making a visit a success or a failure. Cheerfulness, friendliness, and good humour will commend the visitor more than what is said.

5. Enter in the little notebook any details that would be useful to the vicar—names, religion, any children, etc.

6. Pray for your parish. There is enclosed a leaflet of simple prayer.[2]

_____
[2] A suitable one would be S.P.C.K. Tract No. 3253.

AT THE END OF THE MONTH

The books are brought in. Details are copied into the vicar's Visiting Book. He notes cases where he considers a visit by himself is called for, and the visitors have their books returned to them with instructions for the second visit. Obviously they won't go to all the houses next time—some people will have expressed interest but declared themselves Roman Catholic or Methodist, and from other doorways has come the all-purpose rejoinder "Not today, thank you."

Contacts will have been established and the people will realize that the Church is active in their midst and *cares* about them. On the second visit there should be a more detailed invitation to the services or meetings and in some cases a promise to come may be made.

"My hat, Vicar, I shouldn't like your job. At No. 22 they wouldn't answer the door, though you could tell they were in and No. 43 was distinctly rude—the man said he was fed up with canvassers. But I enjoyed it and it makes you think a bit."

We often talk optimistically about our people being evangelistically minded but we shall find that this kind of visiting bristles with difficulties for even the most enthusiastic of our congregations. What is certain is that even if the "Mission" is a failure in terms of numbers, it can do untold good to those who do the visiting beforehand.

In most cases it will be found best to have the teams of visitors going "two by two" and for them to have something in their hands when they go to a house—a leaflet, a parish magazine, an invitation. After the first visit, barriers have been broken down, the people at No. 27 know what the callers are about, and conversation comes more easily. The invitation to "come to church" must in most cases be made —a challenge to each family to stir themselves from the rut of apathy, nominalism, or carelessness into which circumstances may have forced them. The challenge *must* be made in a kindly way; there ought to be nothing judgemental about the invitation so that the people visited are given the impression that they are living in spiritual squalor compared with the heavenly light which people who go to church enjoy. Our visitors go as shepherds sharing in the pastoral work of the caring church.

In many cases this kind of intensive visiting by lay people in preparation for a parochial mission or any kind of "effort" can be merged into a "street warden" system by which each neighbourhood in a parish can be cared for by one or two individual lay people who are responsible for the dissemination of information to the people—parish magazines, leaflets, etc.—and for the transmission to the parish priest of information about sickness, bereavements, potential confirmation candidates, etc. It can become an integral part of the parish intelligence system.

"MAKING OURSELVES HEARD"

The huge Victorian church in a town in East Lancashire was packed to the doors for the final Eucharist of the fortnight's mission. The Bishop, fairly new to the diocese, looked somewhat taken aback when he came into church. He had not really been prepared for this kind of thing. When he gave his address, excellent though it was in its measured sentences and theological rightness, his words seemed completely inappropriate to the occasion. The missioner, who had sweated away for a fortnight, putting everything he had got into the addresses, using simple tableaux and demonstrations of the sacramental life, employing every trick he had learnt from other and greater missioners, felt sick and disappointed. There was no excitement here, no "challenge".

He remembers the bewildered face of the Bishop as they reached the end of administering Holy Communion to over 700 communicants. And he remembers the silver cigarette case which was presented to him some months later by a

grateful P.C.C. But he remembers more uncomfortably the
man who wrote to him later saying that he had been un-
impressed by the mission services but the final service and
the Bishop's address had finally clinched the matter for
him and "he'd come back to his religion".

It is not for us to calculate the results or the returns from
our "making ourselves heard". Surely the Holy Spirit will
dispose of all that. God's "frozen people" can be incor-
porated into the pastoral task of the priest which sooner or
later will involve what is perhaps technically known as
"evangelism". True pastoral care can never be anything else
but evangelistic—and the whole Body of Christ shares in the
Master's Pastorate.

9

We visit as Prophets

"[Christ] . . . after he had made perfect our redemption
by his death, and was ascended into heaven, sent abroad
into all the world his Apostles, Prophets, Evangelists, Doctors, and Pastors, by whose labour and ministry he gathered
together a great flock in all the parts of the world."[1]

There are many ministries which the Holy Spirit raises up
within the Family of Christ's Church; the function of the
apostolic minister is to hold the family together, to stand at
the centre of the life of the apostolic community, to be the
focus of its prophetic ministry as well as its pastoral ministry; and the Church *is* prophetic because it is the Body of
Christ and Jesus Christ is the Prophet *par excellence*.

The function of the Christian minister-prophet is not to
be just a pale imitation of the Old Testament prophet. The
old prophets spoke of a future time when the Spirit of the
Lord would be poured out on all flesh: the Christian priest,
sharing in the prophetic ministry of the whole Church, takes
up the proclamation made by the Apostles that Messiah has
come, died, and risen again and that the Spirit has been
given.

This proclamation is not to be merely an *announcement*
of "religious" events and facts: it is to be a *declaration* of a
new unity in creation which is "not a unity solely of
prophets agreeing in consentient witness to foreshadow the
Christ along one line of revelation; it will be a unity, rather,

[1] From the *Ordering of Priests* in the Book of Common Prayer.

5

of prophets with priests, of poets with law-givers, of devotees with chroniclers, of wise men with story-tellers, and of all these again with rabbis, seers, and philosophers, and with plain men of action."[1]

Quite simply, a priest must "have something to say" not only about the gospel which he is authorized to preach but also about the world which Christ came to redeem. In all his pastoral visits his function is not only that of a listener to the voice of the world but also that of a prophet in the world.

In our visits to people's homes we shall talk much and we shall listen more. It may be that on our first visit we shall talk about little more than the weather and the latest news, but we shall declare the all-embracing love of God by our interest in their affairs, their difficulties, and their fears. There need be no artificial and self-conscious "putting in a word for God", but if we are really humble we shall find ourselves declaring the Word of God in countless ways.

THE PARISH PROPHET

If one talks to old Joe down at the "Five Bells" it will be discovered that *his* idea of "prophecy" will be one which is inextricably related to Old Moore's Almanack, the daily predictions of the astrologer in his favourite newspaper, and the remarkable prowess of a friend of his who won the Treble Chance by using his Army number as guidance in filling up his pools coupon. But he also has a kind of superstitious awe for the "prophetic" powers of the last Rector but one, who once said that there would come a time when two neighbouring parishes which were at daggers drawn would become one. "And it's happened only just recently, you know, Rector: we all said it could never happen, but the old Rector was a prophet, you know."

---

[1] L. S. Thornton, *Revelation and the Modern World*, Dacre Press, pp. 235 f.

We shall never persuade old Joe now that prophecy in the Christian sense is concerned with the present, that it is "an inspired interpretation of, or insight into, present facts, rather than a process of reading the signs and foretelling the future".[1] But we shall go on patiently, in what may seem humdrum ways, exercising our prophetic ministry in our pastoral care.

Old Joe has passed to his rest, but we shall still go into the "Five Bells", not in order to prove that we are broadminded or in order to gain popularity or to acquire another platform for the exposition of our views, but firstly because the "Five Bells" is in our "cure", secondly because the landlord is a friend of ours whose wife has just had an operation and sent a message for her husband when we went to see her in hospital, and thirdly because it is a place where one can exercise one's ministry of listening.

"Good evening, Rector. How are things?"

"Not so bad. How are you? Your wife sent her love and would you take her reading glasses."

"I'll send them up with the boy—can't get there tonight myself. It's Darts Club night and I've no help."

"I won't offer to help myself—I should get all the prices wrong."

"Frank here was just saying he'd like to know what you think about all this space business. Do you think it's a waste of money sending chaps to the moon and so on?"

"Well, I'm no scientist and I'm no economist, but it seems to me that it raises the whole question of how we ought to use any of our money or possessions. . .".

And so the discussion will develop almost artlessly. The priest will be exercising his prophetic ministry in no less powerful a fashion than if he were fulminating from his pulpit.

[1] Martin Thornton, op. cit., Essay 9, "1984".

It will need a good deal of patient spade work and knocking at doors and winning of people's confidence before this kind of "reasoning together" is possible, whether it be in public house or the parlour of "Chez Moi" on the new housing estate. It would seem that some younger clergy are so desperately anxious to fulfil their prophetic ministry that they only see themselves as being able to do this *outside* the usual parochial framework. What we would suggest is that it is possible and practicable to be what could perhaps be called a "minor prophet" *inside* that framework—even, it may be, in spite of it.

HOW THE WORLD THINKS OF US

The Vicar is working through the latest Church Assembly report. The telephone rings: it is a reporter from a local news agency. "Oh, Vicar, I hope you can spare a minute or two. We're very interested here in what one of our local correspondents has told us. Apparently, one of the public houses in your parish is organizing a beer-drinking contest on St Valentine's Day—they say it is an attempt to revive the community spirit and an old English custom centred on the tavern . . . I wonder if you have any comment to make?"

What shall the Christian prophet say? If he says that he thinks it is deplorable that intemperate drinking on this scale should be encouraged (twenty pints of beer is the predictable consumption by some competitors) he knows the sort of headline he will see in the newspapers the following day—"Vicar lashes organizers of beer-drinking contest" or "Vicar hits out" (or "Rector raps"). . . . The organizers will be secretly pleased, as it will give them added publicity and encourage a larger number of curious sight-seeing customers. On the other hand, if he is cautious and merely says that he is in favour of anything which will encourage the community spirit, he knows from experience that the reporter will probably use the eye-catching headline, "Vicar backs beer-drinkers."

"But why do you think that *my* views or the Church's reaction to this sort of thing would be important?" There is an embarrassed silence on the telephone; then the reporter replies warily, "But my readers are always interested in the Church's attitude towards things like this." The Vicar says (rather testily, it must be admitted), "But why are you only interested in occasions when you think you might get a story about us condemning something or disapproving of something?"

"Well, Vicar, I'm afraid our business is *news* and the only news we usually get from the church is when it's condemning something."

The Old Testament prophets were fiery enough in their denunciations of evils and infidelities but were equally eloquent in their proclamation of truth and human worth and nobility. We must be no less fearless in our prophetic ministry, but at the same time no less generous in our positive proclamation of the truth about God's loving relationship to man. And this truth is often conveyed by a humble pastoral relationship with people—the roles of pastor and prophet are interrelated.

10

We visit as Servants

For what we preach is not ourselves but Jesus Christ
as Lord, with ourselves as servants for Jesus' sake.[1]

The form of the Servant casts its shadow backwards from
the incarnate life of Christ through the story of Israel into
the obscure beginnings of history and forwards into the
lineaments of the Bride of Christ. And it is the form in
which God took human flesh and restored our humanity to
wholeness in Christ; it is still the form in which the image of
God restored is still reproduced in the Church, the holy
community. All Christians share in this function because
they are members of a "Servant Church", whether they are
archbishops or train drivers, monks or ballet dancers. We
are all called to "minister", to be of service to other people
in the kind of way which may serve their truest well-being,
to be their "servants".

The ordained ministry shares this responsibility and this
vocation to be a servant, but in a particularly concentrated
and articulated way. The clergy have special functions
which they are authorized to perform by virtue of their
ordination, but there is implicit in their very role the spirit
of diakonia, the meaning of which is set forth by St Luke in
Chapter 22, v. 27: "I am in the midst of you as he that
deacons."

There is much misunderstanding today amongst clergy
about what their position and function in the Church

[1] 2 Cor. 4.5.

really represent. "Anything the priest can do the layman can do better" appears to be the war cry of much radical theology. But when it is analysed and seen in the light of the re-thinking which has taken place in recent years about the structure of the Church and the dignity of lay membership of the Church, some of our fears may be seen to be groundless.

What we shall suggest in this chapter is that the parish priest may fulfil his pastoral ministry to his own people in a more effective way in so far as he sees that ministry as a sharing in the servanthood of Christ. Sometimes we are very much discouraged by all the seemingly profitless goings-on of the institutional Church: sometimes we are maddened by all the "serving of tables" (although that is a very respectable kind of ministry!) which life as a parish priest entails. Many young priests have felt that service as a probation officer or hospital orderly or welfare officer will provide more opportunities for Christian service than "organizing jumble sales and bingo sessions". No doubt God is speaking to the Church through these protests, but, to quote Canon Sydney Evans, "While the parochial system is and will become increasingly artificial in the great conurbations, it is still a viable unit of Christian ministry and certainly in parts of the country it still expresses a natural community. These growths of the centuries aren't just going to disappear overnight."[1]

THE PASTOR AS SERVANT

"What have you got this afternoon, darling?"

"A funeral at 2.30. Cremation afterwards, so I shan't be able to pick up Catherine."

"Well, it will do her good to walk for a change—and it will be still quite light with British Standard Time or whatever it is."

[1] *Ourselves Your Servants* by Sydney Evans, Basil Moss, and Monica Furlong (C.I.O. 1967), p. 18.

"Should be back about 4.30."

"Don't you get bored with riding to the crematorium?"

"Sometimes I feel it's a waste of time—but you can read or talk to Arthur, if he is driving."

"Must you do it?"

"I think I must in this case. It's Mrs B's father."

"Why? Pillar of the church or something?"

"No, but she did say, when she saw the undertaker, she'd 'always got good service' from St Mary's. I told you— remember?"

The details of this actual conversation will no doubt infuriate many clergy. The experts on time and motion study will lament the fact of so many hours being wasted; the economist will calculate that a guinea for this mournful duty is hardly equitable; the rigorist priest will question the right of the parishioner to use her parish church at all as she had never darkened the doors of the church since her mother's death and never subscribed anything towards its upkeep.

And "given good service"—that sounds like a butcher's shop or a television engineering firm. How puerile to suggest that this is a pastoral opportunity! But might not a parish priest remember with profit the incident in the Upper Room when our Lord washed his disciples' feet and said to them, "Know ye what I have done to you? Ye call me Master and Lord; and ye say well; for so I am. If I then, your Lord and the Master, have washed your feet, ye also ought to wash one another's feet. For I have given you an example, that ye should do as I have done to you".

A Christian priest shares in his Lord's "mastership"; he is a teacher, a prophet, a "person" who wields authority in the flock as a pastor. But he is also a minister, a servant. So the "pastoral opportunity" provided by Mrs B's bereavement is an occasion, first and foremost, for the priest to exercise his servanthood, *not* for him to exploit the oppor-

tunity to bring back Mrs B to the fold, as represented by
the local congregation worshipping each Sunday, and by the
Free Will Offering Scheme to which faithful church sup-
porters belong. These things may take shape as a result of
our ministry—we should be poor priests if they didn't—but
that should not be the intention behind our readiness to
minister to particular (and often peculiar) needs.

The more exalted our conception of the priesthood, the
more readily shall we see the necessity for believing that to
be a shepherd of souls involves one in being "the servant of
all". Government and pastorship are very close to one
another. The shepherd must guide and warn and reprove
and encourage, but he cannot rightly do all these things
unless he is giving his life for the sheep and accepting the
limitations to "status" which taking the form of a servant
entails.

"STATUS SEEKERS"

There is much bewilderment in the Church today amongst
its ordained ministers about the role they play, or are
expected to play, or indeed are paid to play, in the various
spheres of ministry. Nor is this puzzlement merely confined
to "unsuccessful" parish priests who are floundering in a
sea of uncertainty caused by the failure of a particular kind
of experiment. We are told by Christian sociologists who
work in close association with the clergy that they have
found it extraordinarily difficult to elicit from the clerical
side of their inquiries into social questions exactly what a
priest sees himself as doing in any particular situation. He
tends to see himself and to act as a sort of gadfly, darting
about from this situation to that problem, talking about "a
Christian presence" in this or that institution or industry,
and imagining that somehow he supplies it.

His role cannot be described in any other than the traditional terms: Priest, Pastor, Prophet, and Servant. But
many people are still going to "have a go" at us. Miss
Monica Furlong, in an address given to the Wakefield

Diocesan Clergy Conference in April 1966, said: "Throughout this century the clergyman has suffered a decline in
status. This is indicated as well as accentuated by the fact
that his income is frequently less than that of his parishioners. In an age which is not particularly interested in
faith it is difficult for people to understand what the clergyman is up to, and so they are apt to suggest that he isn't up
to anything in particular. He isn't a success as the twentieth
century understands success, and his income will not allow
him to enter the status race."

Some readers will feel mounting anger and indignation
as they read this kind of thing, and we shall all search in
our minds and memories for instances in our experience, or
in "my" parish, which will rebut this sort of "defeatist"
writing. But do we really *want* that kind of "status" which
pundits declare we have lost?—large rectories and acres of
glebe with the parishioners touching their caps to us? The
ministry of priest or minister is just the same as ever it was
—to be a pastor or shepherd and also *to be a servant*. The
concept of the "servant" has perhaps been insufficiently
explored in our parochial tradition and there is scope for
further thinking and exposition on the part of theologians;
it may be that we have a lot to learn from other professions
where men and women have little "status" at the beginning
of their careers. They have to be prepared to be servants,
even "dogsbodies"—a priest must be equally so prepared;
then with patience and humility he creates for himself and
his office a "status" which cannot be defined by Statute or
Measure or remunerated by grading or salary scale.

This is not to say that we should despise all the efforts that
are made by the much maligned Church Commissioners
and diocesan officials to improve scales of remuneration. It
is a spurious kind of spirituality which professes a content-
ment with things as they are and would condemn the clergy
to a perpetual necessity of pleading poverty. But the
pastor-prophet-servant will never fit into a convenient slot
in regard to either status or salary bracket; people will never

comprehend entirely what we are up to. It may be that Monica Furlong shares this incomprehension, but we should be wise to listen to what she says later in her address: "I cannot speak for other laymen, but I am clear what I want of the clergy. I want them to be people who can dare, as I do not dare, and as few of my contemporaries dare, to refuse to work flat out (since work is an even more subtle drug than status), to refuse to compete with me in strenuousness. I want them to be people who are secure enough in the value of what they are doing . . . to be the sort of people from whom I can learn some kind of tranquillity in a society which has almost lost the art."

It is in our day-to-day parish visiting that we have a unique opportunity of showing forth these qualities without parading them self-consciously. Nobody else can do what the parish priest is able to do—and this does not apply only to our duties inside a church building.

"YOU MUST HAVE THE 2s. 1½d."

The Vicar looked at the scribbles on the pad on his desk which reminded him that Miss B could do with a visit. He had not been to see her for a few weeks, but he had had messages from her through the parish magazine distributor. She was an eccentric recluse who had come down in the world. She had lived alone in a little house with only outdoor sanitation for 52 years: the interior had not seen a coat of paint or an inch of wallpaper during that time: after suffering with a broken hip for some time she could only struggle with difficulty from bed to commode to armchair to gas stove. All attempts to persuade her to go into an old people's home had failed—she lived in gallant loneliness, assisted only by a home help who came most days to tidy up, to empty her ashes and her slops.

He walked to the house, knocked on the door and pushed it open, shouted, and walked in. He passed through the front of the house, which was as cold as the grave, tapped on the door of the back room and gently opened it. Miss B was asleep in her chair; there was no fire in the grate but dead ashes spewed all over the hearth. A teapot and half a loaf of bread were on the table and a pungent smell betrayed the fact that the commode was almost full. The old lady started out of her sleep, recognized the vicar and began to retail her catalogue of woes. Her home help hadn't been for three days and she couldn't get to the telephone at the bottom of the street to ring up about somebody else. Did the vicar think he could ring up for her? The Vicar thought he could, but before he did that he would clear up a bit. He cleaned out the grate, lit a fire, got the coal in, carried the slop bucket to the W.C. at the bottom of the garden, and washed up.

After that the two of them sat down and sampled a bottle of sherry which the old lady had just had sent by a nephew. As the priest was leaving, Miss B solemnly pressed 2s. 1½d. into his hand and said: "Now that's for you; you did what the Home Help should have done—and don't you dare put it in the church collection." Gravely the priest accepted it and went his way.

Miss B is now in Paradise and is doubtless chuckling at the strange attitudes which cause *us* to chuckle at the events of that afternoon some months before she died; the remarks of her neighbours that it was shocking to ask a vicar to do that sort of thing and that it didn't seem right to see a parson carrying slops down the garden have no doubt caused endless mirth in the heavenly places.

Miss B too is able to see right through the questionings and doubts of a theological student who is reading this and saying to himself, "All we do as ministers of the Gospel, then, is a sort of ambulance work". She is able to contemplate the self-justifying attitudes of Christian ministers with quiet amusement and to consider the strange reasons why the story of that afternoon should be included in a handbook for those just beginning their priesthood of pastoral compassion and servanthood.

11

We visit as Listeners

"I thought I was going to get a sermon."

Together with what is generally called "routine visiting" there is also in any parish priest's experience many an instance of what might be termed "crisis visiting"—that is, if he keeps his ears and eyes open and knows his parish. We may be told of some case of depression or attempted suicide in the parish: some unhappiness which the people concerned do not want to discuss. In some cases we may feel that it would be wrong to intrude, imprudent perhaps in other cases. To act on hearsay is always dangerous, but there are still many occasions when we ought as pastors to go to a house. Our approach should be courteous and friendly.

A reliable Street Warden who didn't go in for gossiping told the Rector that Mr S down the Valley was hitting the bottle. The Rector knew Mr S by sight but had never been in his house. He thought a great deal about this and then decided to make a few visits in the same street as Mr S's and arrived at his doorstep at about 5.45 p.m. The noise of an altercation inside the house suggested to the nervous pastor that this was hardly the time to come.

He knocked and after a minute the door was flung open.

"Good God, it's the bloody parson. What's he come for? I suppose you sent for him, you lying bitch."

"Oh, I'm sorry, Rector—he's drunk again. He can't control himself."

"Well, may I come in?"

The man was drunk, the wife was having an affair with a man at work, there was great unhappiness together with financial problems, deceit, and all the other factors which are so familiar to those who deal with this sort of situation. The Rector felt helpless and hopeless as he stood there, the words, that is the words he felt he ought to be saying, refused to come.

After a time he was asked into the house: for an hour and a half he listened to accusation and counter-accusation. The priest began to feel rather like an umpire in a verbal boxing-bout. He said very little: he finds it impossible as he writes this to remember what he did say. All he knows is that he *listened* and that when he left the house, the man said "Thank you very much for all that—I thought I was going to get a lecture".

Time and time again the priest had an almost instinctive urge to talk about repentance and restitution and loyalty and grace. He had wanted to *solve the couple's problems for them*. But in view of what happened later to the couple he knows now that he probably fulfilled his role of pastor more effectively by listening than by opening his mouth.*

Why is it that in so many cases the last person to be told about an illegitimate baby or a court case is the parson of the parish—told, that is, by the people concerned? Perhaps it is because we are so anxious not to appear to condone sin and wrongdoing that our people think of us as judges rather than shepherds.

Gordon E. Harris in *A Ministry Renewed* cogently reminds us

> of the basic pastoral task, which is that of listening and opening up channels of communication which have become blocked or were, perhaps, never opened. Any pastoral contact, however, trivial, may prove to be the point of departure for helping a sufferer in depth. In the first instance, the parishioner may present the basic prob-

---

* cf. Luke 24, vv. 13ff.

lem in the guise of some lesser and more trivial problem. The church attender who has unaccountably given up churchgoing may, in fact, be appealing for pastoral care. This phenomenon is in line with what is known today about the different levels at which people communicate their deepest needs and longings. Rarely are these needs and longings verbalized; in fact, it is the inability to verbalize them that creates the problem in the first place. The ability to verbalize one's feelings depends upon the establishment of trust between speaker and listener. It also depends upon lowering the level of censorship in a personal relationship to the point where the speaker can express what he really feels without fear of rejection by the listener. For it is precisely this fear of rejection which ensures the persistence of neurotic guilt within the personality long after the original guilt-provoking situation has passed into oblivion.[1]

The insights of modern psychotherapy are not irrelevant to the pastoral task of the Christian minister as he stands on the doorstep of 99 Lobelia Avenue.

[1] Gordon E. Harris, *A Ministry Renewed*, S.C.M., 1968, p. 68.

12

We visit in the Country Parish

"The trouble is—he doesn't understand us."

It is a very tragic fact that in almost every case a clergyman's first curacy is in a town parish. His training is geared to the life and activities of an urban ministry and yet it is highly probable that he will end his days in a country parish, because, as is well known, 40% of the clergy deal with 11% of the population in England; and the vast majority of this 11% live in the country villages.

The highly complex problem of deployment of clergy is one which, no doubt, will gradually be solved, but for some time to come there will be many instances of incumbents being appointed to livings in the rural areas of our country who are unused to the ways of rural England and who will spend much of their time in pining for the more exciting activities of a town parish. Privately they will say that their abilities are being wasted and that they need larger scope for their talents. They will be despondent about their unsuccessful efforts to establish cathedral-type Evensong or equally bitter about the unwillingness of the country folk to accept liturgical reform.

In many cases, though not of course in all cases, they will feel inhibited about exercising any pastoral or prophetic ministry at all. The country villager's devotion to the churchyard will be dismissed as "ancestor-worship" and there will be only a grudging acquiescence in the age-old ceremonies connected with the Harvest Supper. But if he visits, the country person *can* be a prophet! If he really takes an interest in the village hall, if he really tries to understand the problems of tenant-farmers and all the arguments for and against what the newspaper-reading public knows as "factory-farms", if he serves on the parish council not necessarily as chairman but as an elected member, if he establishes *rapport* with the big landowners and developers, he will not necessarily fill his church but there are many ways in which he may be able to contribute towards the illumination of "secular" situations by Christian insights.

We have known many country priests who have identified themselves with the life of their parishes and been regarded as men of God and priests of the people as well. But we have known many cases, too, where it has become only too obvious to the self-conscious villagers that their pastor had only scant regard for their traditions and sometimes curious ways. "You need immense patience, a very large dose of compassion, and a sense of humour about yourself" a very experienced country priest once said.

TOWN PARSON TO COUNTRY PASTOR

The new Rector had not been in the parish very long. He was visiting a sheep-pen in the Derbyshire hills—it was lambing time. The shepherd, who had spent years in New Zealand, looked at the parson impishly.

"I know these lambs better than you know *your* flock."

"Well, it's true I didn't act as midwife to each one of mine, but I'm *trying* to get to know them."

"I know every one of these sixty lambs and which ewe it belongs to. . . ."

"I don't know how you do it. Do you mark them or something?"

"Some of them, but I can tell them without any marking."

"Do they know you?"

"Of course they do—and I talk to them as well. We have a lot to say to one another."

"What do you talk about?"

"Things in general . . . trying to help them . . . the weather . . . how well they're doing . . . God, I suppose. And I tell you what, there are a lot of things in breeding sheep which you wouldn't approve of."

"Well, what exactly do you mean?"

"We have to do a lot of crossing and line breeding to get the right animal for showing. *You*'d call it incest."

"Yes, I wonder sometimes if we're trying to play about with the laws of nature too much. You hear a lot about this factory farming nowadays."

"They had a thing on the telly about it last Sunday night: some of these folk just don't know what they're talking about. Some of these battery hens have a ruddy sight better life than the old farmyard chickens."

"I'd have a better idea of the whole question if I knew more about it."

"And some of you parsons would have a better idea about people if they visited their parishioners a bit more!"

"We're not as thick on the ground as we were, you know."

"That's no excuse. The last chap here was never seen except on Sundays. Always reading books about mysterious theology or something. They tell me he's gone and written a book about us now."

"H'm, yes . . . he was something of a scholar."

"Scholar? I finished being a scholar at the age of ten and a half."

"That wasn't quite what I meant."

"I *like* to go to church . . . I do go occasionally . . . but I like to be recognized when I do go. . . ."

"Yes, but. . . . I haven't seen you there yet myself. . . ."

The Rector suddenly realized he had put a foot wrong. It was not only in church that his vocation to be a prophet could be exercised. He remembered with a pang that the shepherd was not the only person who had not been to church; in fact, there was only a tiny handful of his parishioners he had seen in any of his three churches since his arrival. Although he tried hard to see some signs of life and some signs of sanctifying grace in his new flock, there was little encouragement.

He realized that he had been looking for the same reactions to his ministry which he had come to expect in his town parish. He had been "busy" with many callers, much organization, and many services: he had prepared large numbers of young people for confirmation, there had been many special services for this and that organization and he had been a member of many committees and clubs.

Now he had only 346 people and two churches. Most of them were shy of him, terribly reserved and watching his every move. Although they were no longer isolated in their village and most of the adults went to work in the local town, although they watched television and had their cars and went off on Saturday evenings to eat scampi at the local road-house, they were still a different pastoral problem from the people in the Rector's former cure.

He began the laborious task of visiting them in their homes. He would say that it was from that point that his ministry to his country parish became a real thing.

13

We visit the "Corridors of Power"

"I don't like to trouble you:
I know how busy you are."

Besides the houses in our parishes, there are other buildings
such as offices, factories, schools, police stations, clubs which
we should not neglect. It is not always easy to gain entrance
as a pastor nor should we attempt to storm these citadels
with anything but courtesy and good humour. We do not go
to preach or to condemn or to attempt to "improve" but we
go to show our pastoral concern.

"But how on earth am I to find the time?" When we are
faced, on arrival in our parish, with a forbidding array of
offices and institutions, our first reaction may be that of
panic and a sense of inadequacy. We must be patient: opportunities of making contact with all the agencies which affect
our people's lives and work will inevitably arise as we visit
our homes and get to know our parishioners.

The vicarage door bell had rung at 1.45 p.m. An old man
was standing on the doorstep with an envelope in his hand.
He had had difficulty climbing the steps and was a little out
of breath. The Vicar, who had been having a quick look at
the correspondence columns in the local newspaper, sized
up the situation. He knew the man and recognized the
envelope as being the one which contained the "certificate of
existence" which he signed every twelve months for the old
man: it was from the Government department which paid
him a pension.

The vicar took him into his study and put him in a chair.

He signed the form carefully and tried to be just as neat as the old man was with his painfully contrived signature. "Got arthritis bad, you know, vicar." They chatted about this and that: the old man stumbled to his feet, slowly dragged on his woollen gloves, and said he must be going.

"I'll post this for you, Mr. Jones."

"Oh, that's kind of you. I've put a stamp on. I don't like troubling you—I know how busy you are."

"That's all right—it's a pleasure."

"You've got a lot to do. I'll let you get on with it."

The priest sees him out and "gets on with it"—back to his pipe and perusal of the newspaper. It is true that at 2 p.m. he is leaving for the hospital, but he reflects that in fact he is no "busier" than anybody else. In fact, there is no pressing urgency about anything that afternoon. He is master of his timetable and considerably freer than most of his parishioners.

SERVUS PASTORUM

The most frightening thing about our lives as parish priests is the weight of responsibility that lies on our shoulders of using our time and servanthood, first of all in our worship and prayer, and secondly (and less definably) in our service of and for other people. Whether or not we feel inclined to take Evensong or a funeral—if it has been arranged, we must be there. If we have arranged to take sick communion to somebody, we must be there; if we are in the curriculum at the local school for religious instruction, we shall be there.

But there is no fixed obligation for us to act as servants to all the many agencies which now serve the welfare of the people of our nation; and to many priests the very idea of this may seem strange and unspiritual. What we would suggest is that a priest should see himself as *servus pastorum* in the new situation where the Welfare State has taken over many of the compassionate duties which were once the concern of the Church. In education, in hospitals, in the care of the sick and aged, in the appointment of welfare officers and personnel departments, the State and industry have accepted a pastoral role which we, as priests, should welcome. We may sometimes have our reservations about method, and we may rightly lament the passing of some of the old voluntary agencies; but please let us not be curmudgeonly about our acceptance of a new situation.

There is the now well-known story of the elderly clergyman who bewailed the developments in the Welfare State's care of the sick, when he shook his head and said, "Of course, they always used to come to the rectory to borrow bedpans in the old days: now I *never* see them." Points of contact have doubtless been lost, but immense opportunities have taken their place.[1]

WE NEED NOT ALWAYS BE CHAIRMAN

A parish priest is so accustomed to taking the chair at every meeting in his parish that sometimes he feels a little out of place when he is just another committee member. He is so used to organizing things in his own parish that he feels he must take charge in every other enterprise in which he becomes engaged. If a welfare officer seeks his advice or help about a certain person in his parish who is having domestic problems or financial troubles, the first thing that often comes into the priest's mind is "Why did they not come and see me first?" Worse still, he may resent the welfare officer's "intrusion" into the affairs of his people. It may be that we shall become quite expert in unravelling the intricacies of the regulations hatched out by the Ministry of Social Security, but surely we should let the expert himself do his

[1] For an account of Social Services in Britain today, see Kathleen Jones, *The Compassionate Society*, S.P.C.K. 1966; Jean Heywood, *Casework and Pastoral Care*, S.P.C.K. 1967.

pastoral job, offering our help and guidance. It is our experience that officials do listen if approached in the right way, and it has even been known for them to change their minds!

In our relations with doctors and the medical services we should not assume that we have something to give which other agencies are incapable of giving. Patients may be members of our flocks, but they are the doctor's sheep as well. If right relations are established between ourselves and the local practice, medical care in our parishes will be not only curative but preventive as well, because we shall be able to talk to our medical colleagues about Mrs X who says she won't go to the doctor's but who obviously needs to, and the doctor will be able to commend to us old Mr Y who is suicidal and needs someone to talk to in order to keep him cheerful. We shall accept such a commendation in the spirit of servanthood and not imagine that we are acting as psychiatric colleagues.

In many of our contacts with other welfare agencies we shall find ourselves searching for an identity. Am I doing this as a priest or as a welfare officer or just as a "do-gooder"? We shall waste a lot of time and a lot of emotional energy in worrying about such factors. It is in the idea of servanthood that we shall find the answers to our queryings.

The writer must acknowledge his debt to Canon Basil Moss, who unknowingly acted as a catalyst to provoke some of the things which have been said in this chapter. He was speaking at a meeting in Sidney Sussex College at Cambridge in 1967. He said something which we cannot remember with any accuracy, but what he has written in *Ourselves your Servants* sums up graciously what he then said:

God-given leadership of creativity is always done as the incarnate Lord did his—as a servant. Ministry never ceases to bear its overtone of *diakonia*. This is true of all functions of the ministry to the Church, including pastoral care and the discipline of Christ, sound counsel in con-

fusion and moral mess, the pioneering of prayer. They
are best done by God and set apart by the Church to do
them. If they are to be part of the ministry of Christ, they
must be done as love-in-action, as a washing of feet: for if
God is love is the heart of the Christian perspective, this
must be acted out in servanthood, and not just pro-
claimed.[1]

Then, how *can* the ordinary parish priest's seemingly
pointless visits to the "corridors of power" in his parish be
effective? What is the point of his "busy-ness". Firstly, he
can make friends with those in positions of strength: the
leaders of the community, the officials of the local authority,
the industrialists, the landowners, the Trades Union
officials, the local M.P., and the prospective candidates, and
so on. Out of friendship should develop trust; out of trust
should develop not necessarily co-operation but, it is to be
hoped, at least consultation. It may be that we shall be wel-
comed as welfare officers at first: we should be prepared for
that, but, if we persevere in our quiet servanthood with no
concern for status, we may discover that we are supplying
the Christian insights, without any publicity, for the
formulation of policies in the places where decisions are
made.

On the whole, it is true to say that our people do not
want their priest to be a welfare officer, no matter how
highly trained. They want him to be something different,
someone they can trust about anything in the world,
whether it be the sewage works or their overdraft, their way-
ward daughter or their noisy neighbours. They know "he's
a busy man", although they may not know what he's up to.
But they know he is different and they would like him to
look different. That is why they always feel uncomfortable
when they discover that the man in the collar and tie is
really a priest; they feel taken in and somehow let down.

[1] *Ourselves Your Servants* by Sydney Evans, Basil Moss, and Monica
Furlong (C.I.O. 1967), p. 36f.

Perhaps we may quote what that person of extraordinary sartorial taste, the disc jockey Jimmy Savile, had to say on this subject. A year or two ago he was invited to address a group of young people at a religious meeting. "They'd never heard anything like it. I was honest with them. I told them all about sex and drugs, and the dangers. I didn't mince words. And they believed me." After that he toured the country talking to youth groups, sixth formers, religious organizations.

I went to talk to this group of Anglican priests at a conference [he said] and half were in dog-collars and half in ordinary clothes. And a priest in a sports jacket stood up and asked me what I thought of priests who didn't wear the dog-collar and I looked him straight in the slits and said, "A bit suspect". And he says, "Oh, and why, might I ask?", and I says: "Because if ever I were man enough to be a priest I'd be so proud of my uniform that I'd never take it off. I'd sleep in it, proud to be doing our Lord's work. I'd wear it all the time, because I might be walking down the street, and someone who is in trouble might see me and talk to me. That way I could help. But if I were in ordinary clothes, that troubled person wouldn't recognize me and it would be my fault through disguising myself.[1]

He went off in his own disguise—huge, dark glasses and a teddy bear coat over a scarlet cardigan and blue and white striped trousers. "Basically I'm crazy", he said. It may be so, but it also may be true that he has something to teach us about humility and servanthood.

"I'm sorry, Vicar, but the Managing Director is in conference and the Personnel Officer is busy with interviews—but they say you are quite welcome to go in and see the men in the canteen. Mr X said you might do something about the language there!"

[1] *Sunday Times*, 14 January 1968.

We have not been "snubbed" when this sort of thing happens; it can be the beginning of a very fruitful pastoral relationship.

"I'VE JUST COME OUT OF PRISON"

We are told that there is a kind of "Good Food Guide" circulating by word of mouth amongst the floating community which spends its time on the roads of our country and impinges with great regularity on the parsonages and presbyteries of the church:

A. This one is good for a dollar. Go in the late evening or you'll get some gardening.

B. Depends if he's in. Wife's a terror—always talks about the Welfare State. Usually get a lecture, but gives you a note for the local snack bar.

C. Watch out for dogs here. Once got a pound on Easter Monday. Always wants to see employment card.

D. This one never turns anybody away but never goes above two bob. Doesn't like sight of blood—so don't undo bandages.

E. O.K., but don't say you're Irish or he will send you down road to R.C. church.

It is easy to become cynical about the stream of callers at one's door; the stories of hard luck, cruel fortune, and sheer human misery and deceit become so familiar that one is tempted to dismiss all attempts to raise a loan or to scrounge a meal as confidence tricks. We shall be deceived on many occasions and often we shall feel inadequate as we give the man who "has just come out of prison" five shillings and our blessing: we shall feel, "Is there nothing society can do for men like him?"

We should talk to our local police officers and the officials at the Ministry of Social Security: they need our help just as we need theirs. It is sometimes a help to know that old Paddy who has just been to see us collected over £5 in the town that day. It is comforting to know that there is an interior sprung mattress in one of the new cells at the police station and that "no down-and-out is ever really turned away". Sometimes, on the other hand, it is good for the young police officer to know that it is apparent that an injustice has apparently been perpetrated in the case of young George who had his wallet stolen in the town's lodging house the previous night. Without giving the impression that we are in league with the police we should welcome every opportunity—and seek every opportunity—of serving them. Policemen suffer from a kind of "anticlericalism" in the same way that we do, and they need our friendship; here again a priest can be *servus pastorum*.

14

We visit the "Secular" Organizations

"Our parson is broad-minded: you see
him in pubs and all over the place."

Our pastoral visiting should never be undertaken in order
that we may be described admiringly as "broad-minded" nor
should we delight in hearing people say, "You'd never think
he was a clergyman". But we should never see our "visiting"
as confined to the homes of our parishioners, nor should we
neglect the "secular" organizations or institutions which
come within our pastoral beat.

In days which are seeing much discussion about a "secular-
based theology" it is probably a little dangerous or mislead-
ing to speak of "secular organizations", but it is the most
convenient term we can use to describe the sort of social,
professional, or business organizations with which the parish
priest may be concerned. By the use of the term we are not
"implying a theology of two worlds, where one world makes
a take-over bid for the other",[1] but we are using the term to
outline the various ways in which the parish priest may
become involved with groups of people who are not necessarily members of his congregation.

One can instance such things as clubs of all kinds,
Licensed Victuallers' Associations, Business and Professional
Women's Associations, Women's Institutes, Rotary Clubs,
and the Round Table. What are we to think of ourselves as
we visit these organizations or are asked to help with them?

[1] Simon Phipps, *God on Monday*, Hodder and Stoughton, p. 37.

Supplying a "Christian presence"? Giving the occasion an air of respectability? A person who can say Grace audibly at the Christmas Lunch? Or do we persuade ourselves in the middle of a very lavish "Firm's Annual Dinner" that it is a good thing to be there in case we can slip in a word or two for the Christian Gospel?

Surely it is in these situations that we can most effectually act as Christian pastors and prophets—not by taking advantage of our position to forward the interests of our parish, but by supplying the Christian insights and the pastoral concern for people which we believe the "secular situation" demands.

Once again, the arrangement of our time and the other demands of our pastoral ministry will have to be taken into account before we commit ourselves to the many engagements which will come our way, but there can be no doubt that the parish clergyman will not be wasting his time by speaking (no doubt, on a "secular" subject) at the Townswomen's Guild or by making an after-dinner speech (if he is good at that sort of thing) for the Royal and Antediluvian Order of Buffaloes.

But tell me, what are they going to talk about while snatching a free moment in a pub? Why, about eternal questions: is there a God, is there immortality? And those who do not believe in God? Well, those will talk about socialism and anarchism and the transformation of the whole of mankind in accordance with some new order. So, you see, they're the same damned old questions, except that they start from the other end.[1]

PREACHING GROWS OUT OF VISITING

Some of the things which we have said in this chapter may seem very elementary and to be little connected with our

[1] *The Brothers Karamazov*, Penguin edn., Vol. 1, p. 273.

high-sounding vocation as Christian pastors and prophets,
but

realization of the intimate connection between what we
say and to whom we are saying it will keep us from much
of the pompous, meaningless verbiage which is the scourge
of our apostolate in the pulpit. For every priest and for
every parish, the needs and the consequent adaptations
will be different; by trial and by prayer, and by common
sense, we shall find our own proper approach. Unless we
make that effort we shall go on with our torrent of words,
signifying nothing. Our responsibility is overwhelming.
We are the only ones in the whole of God's world who can
give a meaning to life, who can answer the torturing
doubts and despair of the confused twentieth century;
without the message of Christ which we were ordained to
spread, nothing can halt the growth of self-destruction.
We must do it, for no one else can.[2]

The more we visit in the sort of communities which do
not speak our language or understand it, the more we shall
realize the need in our own preaching of language and
modes of expression which will be more likely to reach the
hearts and minds and consciences of our hearers.

"It takes a man of God to preach the Word of God" and
the true prophet will be a true pastor. True prophecy
demands a passion for souls, a great sorrow at the ills of the
world, and a burning desire to do something—and say
something—about it.

"Know your people, and find out what they are thinking,
and make your entrance from there." (Michonneau)

[2] G. Michonneau, *Revolution in a City Parish*, Blackfriars, p. 144.

15

Visiting is not a Waste of Time

"To live in the midst of the world with no desire for its
pleasures; to be a member of every family, yet belonging
to none; to share all sufferings, to penetrate all secrets, to
heal all wounds; to go daily from men to God, to offer him
their homage and petitions; to return from God to men, to
bring them his pardon and his hope; to have a heart of iron
for chastity and a heart of flesh for charity; to teach and
to pardon, console and bless, and to be blessed for ever. O
God, what a noble life, and 'tis thine, O priest of Jesus Christ."[1]

Lacordaire's description of the pastor's life may frighten us
and it may seem to some that his words apply more to a celi-
bate priesthood and to a different *milieu*. Indeed, the
French, we are told, talk of the priesthood as "the third sex"
—men, women, and priests. But unless the Church has at
the heart of its ministry to the world a priesthood con-
secrated to the pastoral ideals enshrined in this definition of
"the noble life" it is in danger of perishing for lack of vision,
lack of prophecy, and lack of pastoral concern—and all because of our refusal to accept the servanthood which loyalty
to him who was the Good Shepherd involves. Moreover, it is
a matter for fruitful recollection that Jean Baptiste Henri
Lacordaire was one of those who founded the Journal
L'Avenir, which was condemned by the Pope for its
radicalism.

Before we dismiss the words of the Frenchman as being

[1] Lacordaire (1802–1861).

irrelevant to the pastoral situation today, let us recall that ministerial priesthood belongs to no man by right. It is not a reward of any excellence or virtue. We cannot say that the better sort of laypeople are called to the priesthood: it is certainly not true that the more intellectually able are always called to the ministry. Some people may mourn this fact: but at the same time we should try to see what the Spirit is saying to the Church about these things; the call of God sounds with different tones in different generations.

What remains true for all time is that neither the brilliant scholar-priest nor the humble peasant-priest could in any age consider himself worthy of the office to which he has been ordained. Moreover, we should remember that we are only allowed to share the priesthood of Jesus Christ *for the sake of the whole people of God.*

God calls some priests to be monks, to offer their lives and talents in complete dedication to prayer and worship, study and work. God calls other priests to serve him and his people in parishes—and this is the framework in which the majority of us have to exercise our ministry for the sake of the whole people of God: and it is at this point that so many of us feel frustrated and begin to lament the inadequacies of that framework. What we would suggest in all diffidence is that many of us have failed in the matter of stewardship—and, most of all, in stewardship of time.

THE STEWARDSHIP OF TIME

To one who has been long in city pent,
    'Tis very sweet to look into the fair
    And open face of heaven—to break a prayer
Full in the smile of the blue firmament
Who is more happy, when, with heart's content,
    Fatigued, he sinks into some pleasant lair. . . .

                                                  John Keats

For some years the writer occupied part of the house in

which John Keats lived during his days as a medical student at Guy's Hospital. When he wrote this sonnet in 1817 he was a "dresser" to such great surgeons of the day as Astley Cooper and, apart from long sessions in the primitive conditions of the operating theatres, attended lectures which began at eight in the morning and were staggered throughout the day, the last being at eight in the evening. He cannot have had a great deal of leisure in which to write and his duties as a dresser cannot have been anything but distracting in those days when antiseptic surgery was unknown and after operations wounds almost always became infected. A friend of Keats, Henry Stephens, tells us in one of his letters that the poet would occasionally scribble rhymes on his own syllabus or that of a friend during lectures. And out of those noisy and sometimes frantically busy days come the placid words of Keats' poem.

A hospital chaplain, occupying Keats' House, a hundred and forty or so years later, was no less beset by people and activity, and he was tempted to indulge Keats' nostalgia for the countryside. He would picture a rural "reprieve" from the demands of the hospital, although it was not a picture graced by images outlined by any poetic genius such as Keats possessed. He was appalled by the immensity of the task and for the first few months floundered amongst the complexities of establishing priorities. If he stayed in his office, there was a never-ending procession of ne'er-do-wells, down-and-outs, people with real problems both material and spiritual. He was tempted to establish his "surgery" in the basement of Keats' House and to try to exercise his ministry from there.

But the thousand patients in the hospital beds were his primary responsibility—at least, that was the idea of the Ministry of Health which employed him and paid him. And there were the staff and the doctors and the domestic workers and the physiotherapists also needing his care. But how could he assess the different needs? Moreover there were no tangible results of any of his ministrations. There was no account of his stewardship which he could present at an Annual Parochial Meeting with stories of a record number of communicants, confirmations, and baptisms and how the Gift Day had "brought in more than ever before".

Slowly he learnt that it is self-centred vanity which looks for results, that the desire to be an "expert" with one's own list of clients is often the result of unhealthy nostalgia and that the pastor's duty lies primarily towards the people whom God has put into his hands—in parish, hospital, school, regiment, ship, or works.

And, although he would confess to many inadequacies and failures and infidelities, he had to learn something about the stewardship of time. It is our firm conviction that a great deal of the *malaise* in the Church amongst its ministers is due not to the unorthodox prophets or the antique machinery of some of our institutions, but to the lack of pastoral zeal and the seeming inability of many clergy to organize their time efficiently and with *people* in mind.

"THE HOUSE-GOING PARSON MAKES A CHURCH-GOING PEOPLE"

This is often quoted in Pastoralia papers for ordination examinations. Candidates are asked to evaluate the much-used dictum. We have known many cases where the liveliness and devotion of a congregation owed an immeasurable amount to diligent visitation by generations of zealous incumbents. On the other hand there are many cases where the priest "was never out of our houses, even at meal-times" and the church was persistently empty Sunday by Sunday. The purpose of the pastoral visit surely is not to fill one's church—though one may hope to—but to extend Christ's love and care to our people. The old saying may be an exaggeration, but it is no exaggeration to say that church-going people are kept loyal by the priest who takes the trouble to know them in their own homes.

"If they want me, they know where to find me." "It's no use visiting nowadays, they always have the telly on." "It's teaching they want, not visiting—I'm doing part-time teaching at the local school now and I find plenty of opportunities of teaching the faith." "Committee work takes up all my time nowadays, and I do believe that my people would prefer to be left alone." Perhaps we should do better to meditate on the words of the Good Shepherd himself: "He that is a hireling ... fleeth because he is a hireling, and careth not for the sheep. I am the Good Shepherd, and know my sheep, and am known of mine." (John 10.13–14).

THE "IMAGE" OF
THE PARISH PRIEST TODAY

The Parochial Church Council was having one of its regular meetings in the vicarage dining-room. They had moved there because there was a badminton match in the parish hall, the Guides were meeting in the small room of the hall, the vestry was too small (and you could not smoke) and the vicar's study was occupied by a working party addressing envelopes.

The P.C.C. meeting had been concentrating its mental energies on arrangements for the Garden Fete ("Anybody got any new ideas?"), the persistent draught from the front door of the church ("If you sit near the font, you can feel a howling gale round your ears"), and a request from the Urban District Council that they be allowed to take a two foot strip of the churchyard for road widening. Suddenly a late-comer broke into the discussion with, "You know, I was watching a programme on Television last night and I've been wondering exactly what sort of image we present to the people outside the Church. Are we just people concerned with taking in our own washing—fiddling about with draughts and raising money and our own petty little affairs? Don't you think, Vicar, we ought to be more out-going, talking about how we could help that chap next door to me, for instance, who's got a backward son and his wife's left him . . . and I'm bothered about you, too, Vicar, and your image. There was a young chap on the same programme, a priest, I think, but he had a collar and tie on, and he said he was fed up with the image of clergy who just went round having cups of tea with old ladies. . .".

"I think you're absolutely right, Jack", interjected the Vicar, much to the surprise of some of the staider members of the P.C.C. who thought that Jack was guilty of *lèse-majesté* and was out to cause trouble. "But we'll just finish off this business about the churchyard and then we can discuss some of the things you are worried about."

That meeting lasted until a very late hour and the vicar's chop, which had been left in the oven, was burnt so as to be almost inedible. It soon became evident that Jack's outburst was the symptom of a very deep misunderstanding of why the parish church was there at all, but that his compassionate concern for the man next door was something which put to shame the complacency of some of the other members of the Council. And the constant reference to the "image" of the priest and the Church betrayed his acceptance of the view that in order to be valid, respectable, or worthy it is necessary for any institution, policy, or saleable article to have an "image" which may not necessarily be absolutely true in every respect but which public relations experts may have authenticated as being "proper".

Nothing but good came of Jack's outburst at that meeting, but both priest and people came to see that the justification for any action by parson or parish is to be found in its inherent rightness and not in any possibility that the appearance might be good for Christ's Church.

"DO I LOOK LIKE A PARSON?"

Some years ago there was to be seen flapping on a notice-board in a church porch in Suffolk a poster which displayed a rear view of an untidy looking young man. He was looking over his shoulder and saying (according to the caption) "Do I look like a parson?" The villages gazed at this poster as they went into the Church on Trinity Sunday. Some said, "What's it all about? I expect the Vicar will tell us." Others expressed their distaste by shrugging their shoulders and dismissing it as "some of this satire". The Vicar's wife looked at it quizzically and said, "Well, he certainly *does* look like a parson—his suit's so badly cut. But what's it all in aid of?"

"It's supposed to inspire young men to become priests." The Vicar said this with a certain lack of confidence in his voice. He had almost dropped it in the waste paper basket when it had arrived with a request that it should be displayed at Trinitytide, but he had reflected that this was perhaps some subtle advertising technique which he had not been trained to understand. He had heard that experts in public relations had been called in to advise on recruiting posters for the Ministry of the Church and, after all, television advertisements often seemed to be designed to poke fun at the products they sought to promote.

Surely the only form of advertising or promotion which the servant ministry of the church may engage in is the demonstration in terms of servanthood of a priesthood which is both intensely involved in the world in which it is exercised and also deliberately remote from the world of public acclaim and human esteem. The image of the priesthood is closely interwoven with the image of Christ in whose face the world has seen the image of God. And it may be that the priest who was angry at the appearance of that poster was angry for self-regarding reasons. "Knocking" at the clerical profession causes us a certain amount of distaste (after all, we're only human), but if we remember what a respectable ancestry the word "parson" has—the "persona" of Christ in every parish—we have a clue to the role for which so many of us seem to be searching.

Canon Eric James has written:

The Form of the Slave underlies the whole concept of

Christian ministry, even the episcopate. In an affluent and acquisitive society, a society greatly concerned with "keeping up with the Joneses", and concerned too that the vicar shall have a certain dignity and status (because that will add dignity and status to the neighbourhood and the neighbours), it is clear that the separation of the priesthood will mean the Cross, and that the priest will be tempted not only directly by the Tempter within himself, or within his family, but within the congregation and the parish and in society at large.

The Form of the Servant may mean these days, in part, the form of the civil servant, for administration may be a real part of pastorate in a complex society.

For the priest there is in every situation the same prayer to be said, the prayer that was Christ's prayer as he set out from heaven in obedience, and as in the same obedience he laid down his life: "Father, glorify thy name". It is not a cold, sullen, or bitter obedience. It has only one purpose: that those who are separated from God and from each other may be "one, even as we are one". The separation of Christ is in order to end the separation of men; and so, therefore, supremely, is the separation of the priesthood which stems from the priesthood of Christ. Whether it is a political situation, an industrial situation, a parochial situation, or in an educational institution, wherever a priest is, there is a vocational separation if he is fully to enter that world and be there as a reconciler, to end separation. He is there "that they also be with me where I am; that they may behold my glory".[1]

To "one who has been long in city pent" a great deal of what has been said in this book may seem unrealistic. We may even be accused of romanticizing the pastoral situation. Some may feel that what we have suggested is, after all,

[1] Eric James, *Odd Man Out*, Hodder and Stoughton, p. 85.

nothing but a sort of political canvass. It may be felt, too, that we have not taken into sufficient account the questioning in people's minds about the whole concept of God and the validity of the claims of the Christian religion. Or again it may be that those who are labouring in rural parishes where they are able "to breathe a prayer Full in the smile of the blue firmament", will think that we have failed in appreciation of what is involved in maintaining three medieval churches in three decaying villages, in living in an enormous, old (or stupidly small, new) parsonage, with tiny congregations whose ideas are distinctly feudal.

We may have been guilty of exaggeration, but perhaps we may be permitted to ask what other solution to the problems in the present pastoral situation is practicable. We ask this because we believe with Roger Lloyd that

> the emphasis on the pastoral is the only thing which could save the Anglican spiritual economy from the heresy of rating the collective above the individual, of preferring to deal with crowds and herds, of laboriously estimating power in terms of mass trends and tendencies, rather than the dealing with individual people, individual families, and small groups one at a time. That is why the parochial system is the characteristic Anglican device for seeing that for every soul there shall be his own pastor. The Anglican Church is essentially and fundamentally pastoral. It cannot be said too often, for nobody will ever understand Anglicanism who ignores this basic fact. It is always the great pastors who remain beloved heroes for one generation after another. It is possible that Archbishop Laud did more for the Church than George Herbert, but through the centuries it is Herbert who is loved while Laud is at best admired. Those bishops (and priests) are loved best who know their sheep and are known by them. . . .[1]

[1] Roger Lloyd, *The Church of England, 1900–1965* (S.C.M.), p. 21.

Almighty God, give us priests
to establish the honour of thy Holy Name;
to proclaim the faith of Jesus;
to christen and to teach the young;
to tend Thy sheep; to seek the lost;
to offer the holy sacrifice at the altar;
to feed us with Jesus, the Bread of life;
to give pardon to repentant sinners;
to bless our homes; to comfort the afflicted;
to strengthen us in our last hour.
Almighty God, give us priests.

(A.C.S. Prayer)

Postscript

The writer is very conscious that there are many questions which the priest in his own parish will find unanswered in these pages. The use of the latest advances in technology, for instance, in compiling parish records (has not the *New Christian* recently reminded us with amused relish that computers are already in use in the Episcopal Church in the United States of America for checking on the attendance of acolytes at church services?), the necessity for an *ecumenical* approach to pastoral care with a greater sense of mutual commitment between denominations, the overwhelming demand from the younger clergy that there should be more guidance from our leaders and theological lecturers about the more economical use of time and money in the Church— these are all matters about which there must be continuing debate in the years ahead.

The fact that these subjects have been but lightly touched on does not mean that we think them unimportant, but what we have been concerned to argue is that the Anglican heritage of pastoral care which is based on person-to-person encounter in the parish is one that we hold in trust and ought not to abandon lightly.

New patterns of ministry there must be in the years to come, re-deployment and variations in strategy are going to be desperately necessary in the later decades of the twentieth century, but we must be sure that our radical ideas for re-structuring are based not on *arrogance* but on real pastoral love and concern.

We ought to look back and distinguish amongst our own

pastoral achievements—if that is a proper definition—the occasions when we have felt ourselves to be polished shafts in the hands of God. . . . The night we knelt amongst the dying embers of a squalid hearth with an estranged man and wife and at 2.30 a.m. in the morning heard them say "Amen" to our prayer for their forgiveness and reconcilia-tion. It may be that we were only able to do that because we knew them in their homes and had originally visited their house at a neighbour's suggestion. . . . The morning we received telephone messages from a High Court Judge and a telephone operator after a broadcast . . . perhaps we were only able to be prophetic because we had visited them in their homes and were able to speak to their condition. . . . The two days we spent acting as chauffeur to a man whom the doctor had forbidden to drive his grocery van . . . it may be that we were able to take the form of a servant only because we knew him in the surroundings of his own home, his financial circumstances, his fears—and his loyalty.

> Prophecy will fade away,
> Melting in the light of day;
> Love will ever with us stay;
>   Therefore give us love.

Index